IELTS SPEAKING STRATEGIES

The Ultimate Guide With Tips, Tricks, And Practice On How To Get A Target Band Score Of 8.0+ In 10 Minutes A Day

RACHEL MITCHELL

Copyright © 2017

All rights reserved.

ISBN: 9781549720727

TEXT COPYRIGHT © [RACHEL MITCHELL]

all rights reserved. No part of this guide may be reproduced in any form without permission in writing from the publisher except in the case of brief quotations embodied in critical articles or reviews.

Legal & disclaimer

The information contained in this book and its contents is not designed to replace or take the place of any form of medical or professional advice; and is not meant to replace the need for independent medical, financial, legal or other professional advice or services, as may be required. The content and information in this book have been provided for educational and entertainment purposes only.

The content and information contained in this book have been compiled from sources deemed reliable, and it is accurate to the best of the author's knowledge, information, and belief. However, the author cannot guarantee its accuracy and validity and cannot be held liable for any errors and/or omissions. Further, changes are periodically made to this book as and when needed. Where appropriate and/or necessary, you must consult a professional (including but not limited to your doctor, attorney, financial advisor or such other professional advisor) before using any of the suggested remedies, techniques, or information in this book.

Upon using the contents and information contained in this book, you agree to hold harmless the author from and against any damages, costs, and expenses, including any legal fees potentially resulting from the application of any of the information provided by this book. This disclaimer applies to any loss, damages or injury caused by the use and application, whether directly or indirectly, of any advice or information presented, whether for breach of contract, tort, negligence, personal injury, criminal intent, or under any other cause of action.

You agree to accept all risks of using the information presented inside this book.

You agree that by continuing to read this book, where appropriate and/or necessary, you shall consult a professional (including but not limited to your doctor, attorney, or financial advisor or such other advisor as needed) before using any of the suggested remedies, techniques, or information in this book.

TABLE OF CONTENT

Introduction
Ielts Speaking Introduction
Part 1 Speaking Topics
What Will Give You A High Score In The Speaking Part 1?
How Does The Examiner Mark Your Speaking Test?
Part 1 Speaking Essentials
Fluency Markers
Time And Frequency Expressions
Adverbials For Giving Opinions
Part 1 Speaking Practice
Preference Questions
Part 1 Speaking Model Answers
List Of Part 1 Speaking Questions To Practice At Home
Part 2 Speaking Introduction
Part 2 Speaking Tips
People Description
Adjectives Of Personality
People Description Model Answer
Model Sentences For People Description
Place Description
Adjectives For Describing Places
Place Description Model Answer
Model Sentences For Place Description
Object Description
Useful Adjectives For Describing Objects
Object Description Model Answer
Model Sentences For Object Description
Past Event Description
Past Event Description Model Answer
Model Sentences For Past Event Description
Part 3 Speaking Introduction
Language For Giving And Supporting Opinions
Practice Questions
Talking About Advantages And Disadvantages
Hypotheticals
Practice Questions
Proposing Solutions To Problem
Practice Questions
Agreeing And Disagreeing
Language For Expressing Likelihood
The Future Perfect & The Future Continuous

Practice Questions
Model Sentences For Part 3 Speaking
Part 3 Speaking Questions For Practice
Friendship
Successful People
Advertisement
Teaching
Advice
Adventurous People
Animals
Cell Phones
Computers
Fashion & Shopping
Gifts
Transportation
Photography
Music
Films
Sports
Food
TV Programmes
Relaxation
Newspapers And Magazines
Parties
Travelling
Noise
Reading
Festivals
Parks
Conclusion
Check Out Other Books

INTRODUCTION

Thank you and congratulate you for downloading the book *"IELTS Speaking Strategies: The Ultimate Guide with Tips, Tricks and Practice on How to Get a Target Band Score of 8.0+ in 10 Minutes a Day."*

This book is well designed and written by an experienced native teacher from the USA who has been teaching IELTS for over 10 years. She really is the expert in training IELTS for students at each level. In this book, she will provide you all proven Formulas, Tips, Tricks, Strategies, Explanations, Structures, Part 1 + Part 2 + Part 3 Speaking Language, Vocabulary and Model Part 1 + Part 2 + Part 3 Answers to help you easily achieve an 8.0+ in the IELTS Speaking, even if your speaking is not excellent. This book will also walk you through step-by-step on how to develop your well-organized answers for the Part 1 + Part 2 + Part 3 Speaking; clearly analyze and explain the different types of questions that are asked for the IELTS Speaking Test; provide you step-by-step instructions on how to answer each type of question excellently.

As the author of this book, Rachel Mitchell believes that this book will be an indispensable reference and trusted guide for you who may want to maximize your band score in IELTS Speaking. Once you read this book, I guarantee you that you will have learned an extraordinarily wide range of useful, and practical IELTS Part 1 + Part 2 + Part 3 Speaking strategies and formulas that will help you become a successful IELTS taker as well as you will even become a successful English user in work and in life within a short period of time only.

Take action today and start getting better scores tomorrow!

Thank you again for purchasing this book, and I hope you enjoy it.

IELTS SPEAKING INTRODUCTION

The IELTS speaking test lasts about 11 to 14 minutes. It has 3 parts, and it's worth 25% of your IELTS score.

However, the speaking test is very unique because it's much shorter than the other sections. Specifically, writing test (1 hour), listening test (45 minutes), reading (1 hour), and speaking test (11-14 minutes).

The IELTS speaking test is shorter but it gives you more opportunities to practice more basic skills.

Let's talk about the three parts of the speaking test.

PART 1 SPEAKING TOPICS

The skills in part 1 speaking are exactly the skills that we need for part 2 and part 3 speaking. So what we need to do in part 1 speaking is we need to focus on building basic skills.

There are two purposes to part 1 speaking. The first purpose is to calm you down. They know that you are nervous, so they're going to ask you simple questions that get you settle down and prepare for part 2 & part 3 speaking (the more difficult parts). The second purpose of part 1 speaking is of course for you to show the examiner your ability to speak English. They want you to calm down and they want you to show the most you can do with your English.

In part 1 speaking, the questions are about **you, your home, your life, your family, or your country**, which are things that you have the answer to. They are not asking you questions like *"who wants to be a billionaire?", "who was the 15th president of the United States?"*. Normally, in part 1 speaking, they will be giving you 3 topics:

The 1st topic: The first topic will always be *"do you work or do you study?"* or *"where you are living?"*

If you answer that you are working, then they will ask you about your work.

If you answer that you are studying, then they will ask you about your study.

The next 2nd and 3rd topics: The next 2nd and 3rd topics can be about **anything**, but it is not going to be a sensitive topic; they are not going to ask you about politics. Instead, they will ask you something about general topics that you have ideas to answer. These things might be about **rain,** for example, *how often does it rain in your country? Or how do you feel when it rains?*. They also might ask you questions about ***movies, colors, hobbies, etc***. These are simple questions, they are not challenging questions, but we cannot easily predict what the examiner will be asking you about.

Here is the thing. The examiner doesn't care about your answer. If they ask you *"do you like to read?"* they don't care if you say *"yes, I love reading"* or *"no, I hate it"*. They don't care, they want to hear *how you communicate*.

WHAT WILL GIVE YOU A HIGH SCORE IN THE SPEAKING PART 1?

<u>Rule Number 1:</u> Answer the question. Make sure you answer the question.

<u>For example:</u> *do you like to read books?*

Well, books are really enjoyable. People like to read books because they find it very relaxing, and they can get a lot of information from books. My father really enjoys reading; and every Friday night, he sits at home with a book and drinks some tea....

Am I answering the question? **No, I am not.**

Definitely, the examiner does know that I <u>did not answer</u> the question because I chose not to. I didn't answer the question.

<u>Rule Number 2:</u> you need to show the examiner something or some things about your English ability, and that can be something about your grammar, something about your vocabulary, something about the organization of your answer, and maybe something about your pronunciation.

We must know that IELTS is a game, and a test is a method with rules that allows you to gain points and lose points. Therefore, in order to be successful with any game and IELTS in particular, we need to <u>know what the rules are</u>, and we need to <u>know how to gain points, **not** lose points</u>.

<u>Example:</u> *"Do you enjoy reading?"*

<u>Answer 1:</u> *Yes, I love to read*

<u>Answer 2:</u> *To be honest, I hate reading. I think it's a stupid hobby. I think people that read are actually very boring and they annoy me tremendously.*

Which answer is better? The first one or the second one? Of course, <u>the second one</u>. Even though the second answer is a bit strange, a bit rude, but that's not what the examiner will mark in the IELTS exam. Good vocabulary, good grammar, good sentence structures; that is what they mark. So, show the examiner your English ability.

Note that **never** give a one-word answer, always use complete sentences or at least complete phrases, and extend your answer by providing some kinds of explanations or descriptions.

For example: *"Do you enjoy reading?"*

Answer: ***"yes"***

Well, if you just give a one-word answer like this, you've got nothing with your pronunciation, nothing with your vocabulary, and nothing with your grammar. You've got nothing.

What you need to do is you need to extend your answer. The big mistake of part 1 speaking that a lot of people make is that they lose sight over how important it is. In fact, speaking part 1 is quite easy. However, most people tend to expect something more difficult in part 1 speaking such as, *"please get me the harder questions? Or "please get me the good questions?"*. But **no**, the questions they give you in part 1 speaking are already the good stuff, and you will see that the way you answer questions in part 1 speaking is exactly what you need for part 2 and part 3 speaking. Therefore, you need to be willing to practice questions for part 1 speaking.

HOW DOES THE EXAMINER MARK YOUR SPEAKING TEST?

You need to know and understand the four categories. Let's take a look at the IELTS speaking band descriptors as below:

IELTS Speaking band descriptors (public version)

Band	Fluency and Coherence	Lexical Resource	Lexical Resource	Pronunciation
9	• speaks fluently with only rare repetition or self correction; any hesitation is content-related rather than to find words or grammar • speaks coherently with fully appropriate cohesive features • develops topics fully and appropriately	• uses vocabulary with full flexibility and precision in all topics • uses idiomatic language naturally and accurately	• uses a full range of structures naturally and appropriately • produces consistently accurate structures apart from 'slips' characteristic of native speaker speech	• uses a full range of pronunciation features with precision and subtlety • sustains flexible use of features throughout • is effortless to understand
8	• speaks fluently with only occasional repetition or self-correction; hesitation is usually content-related and only rarely to search for language • develops topics coherently and appropriately	• uses a wide vocabulary resource readily and flexibly to convey precise meaning • uses less common and idiomatic vocabulary skilfully, with occasional inaccuracies • uses paraphrase effectively as required	• uses a wide range of structures flexibly • produces a majority of error-free sentences with only very occasional inappropriacies or basic/non-systematic errors	• uses a wide range of pronunciation features • sustains flexible use of features, with only occasional lapses • is easy to understand throughout; L1 accent has minimal effect on intelligibility
7	• speaks at length without noticeable effort or loss of coherence • may demonstrate language-related hesitation at times, or some repetition and/or self-correction • uses a range of connectives and discourse markers with some flexibility	• uses vocabulary resource flexibly to discuss a variety of topics • uses some less common and idiomatic vocabulary and shows some awareness of style and collocation, with some inappropriate choices • uses paraphrase effectively	• uses a range of complex structures with some flexibility • frequently produces error-free sentences, though some grammatical mistakes persist	• shows all the positive features of Band 6 and some, but not all, of the positive features of Band 8
6	• is willing to speak at length, though may lose coherence at times due to occasional repetition, self-correction or hesitation • uses a range of connectives and discourse markers but not always appropriately	• has a wide enough vocabulary to discuss topics at length and make meaning clear in spite of inappropriacies • generally paraphrases successfully	• uses a mix of simple and complex structures, but with limited flexibility • may make frequent mistakes with complex structures, though these rarely cause comprehension problems	• uses a range of pronunciation features with mixed control • shows some effective use of features but this is not sustained • can generally be understood throughout, though mispronunciation of individual words or sounds reduces clarity at times

5	• usually maintains flow of speech but uses repetition, self-correction and/or slow speech to keep going • may over-use certain connectives and discourse markers • produces simple speech fluently, but more complex communication causes fluency problems	• manages to talk about familiar and unfamiliar topics but uses vocabulary with limited flexibility • attempts to use paraphrase but with mixed success	• produces basic sentence forms with reasonable accuracy • uses a limited range of more complex structures, but these usually contain errors and may cause some comprehension problems	• shows all the positive features of Band 4 and some, but not all, of the positive features of Band 6
4	• cannot respond without noticeable pauses and may speak slowly, with frequent repetition and self-correction • links basic sentences but with repetitious use of simple connectives and some breakdowns in coherence	• is able to talk about familiar topics but can only convey basic meaning on unfamiliar topics and makes frequent errors in word choice • rarely attempts paraphrase	• produces basic sentence forms and some correct simple sentences but subordinate structures are rare • errors are frequent and may lead to misunderstanding	• uses a limited range of pronunciation features • attempts to control features but lapses are frequent • mispronunciations are frequent and cause some difficulty for the listener
3	• speaks with long pauses • has limited ability to link simple sentences • gives only simple responses and is frequently unable to convey basic message	• uses simple vocabulary to convey personal information • has insufficient vocabulary for less familiar topics	• attempts basic sentence forms but with limited success, or relies on apparently memorised utterances • makes numerous errors except in memorised expressions	• shows some of the features of Band 2 and some, but not all, of the positive features of Band 4
2	• pauses lengthily before most words • little communication possible	• only produces isolated words or memorised utterances	• cannot produce basic sentence forms	• speech is often unintelligible
1	• no communication possible • no rateable language			
0	• does not attend			

1. FLUENCY AND COHESION: The first category that the examiner is marking your speaking is the fluency and cohesion. They will be marking you on:

- Do you speak *smoothly without long pauses*?
- Do you *produce new information*?
- Do you *link your ideas by using fluency markers*?

Fluency markers are words like *"however", "furthermore", "also", "as a result", "consequently", "so", "unfortunately", "for example"*, etc.

You <u>should be fluent</u> not only in part 1 speaking, but also in part 2 and part 3 speaking.

Note that fluency **is not speed** (<u>not too fast</u> and <u>not too slow</u>). Unfortunately, some students are going to hurt their score when they try to speak too fast because their mouth is going too fast to their brain.

2. LEXICAL RESOURCE (VOCABULARY): The second category that we should think about is Lexical Resource. You will be doing a lot of vocabularies in your IELTS speaking:

+ You should use **linking vocabulary**. You should use **words that signal** such as *therefore, so, for example, nowadays, unfortunately, surprisingly, etc.*

+ You should use **topic vocabulary**: vocabulary that we will use for particular topics, for example, *topics about television, movies and books, technology, etc.*

+ You should use **phrasal verbs** *such as, look into, look onto, etc.*

+ You should use a range of words. You **don't** just want to say *"it's really good"*, or *"it's good"*, or *"everything is good"*. You should make your answer better by using a range of synonym words of *"good"*. You can use *"fantastic/ spectacular/ awesome/ tremendous, etc."*

+ You will not get a high score unless you use a wide range of vocabulary accurately, and you do some simple things like *"paraphrasing"*. **Paraphrasing** is when you change the words that they ask you in the question.
For example, if they ask you *"do you like to read?"* You **should not** say *"yes, I love to read."* Although your grammar is ok, but if you want to get a better score you **should say** *"yes, I love reading"*. Certainly, you will get a better score because you have changed the verb form. Or you can say *"yes, I love doing that"*.

When you start to learn vocabulary words, it's really good to build vocabulary as you keep going, as you keep studying, but you don't have to sit down and try to study about 20 vocabulary words. Instead of doing that, it's better if you try to only learn may be 1 or 2 words at a time, and then immediately start using the words. Don't learn a list of 10 words, and then think *"oh, I've just learnt the 10 words"*. You shouldn't do that. What you should do is to learn 2 words a day and start using those words right away by using those words often in sentences, then you will find that you learn words more deeply, and the more you do it, the quicker your brain processes new vocabulary.

Idioms: The other thing you should do if you want to get a higher score (7.0+) is that you need to be able to use a range of **idioms**. Idioms are phrases that don't mean exactly what they sound what they mean, for example, *"raining cats and dogs", "become green with envy", "cost an arm and a leg",* *"sleep like a baby"*. **Idioms** are very challenging, and this is the one thing that almost students do not use in the final test. Why? Remember that when the examiner asks you certain questions, they are inviting certain answers. For example, if they ask you *"would you like to travel to another country?"*

Note that, if the examiner asks you a question with the modal verb *"would"*, they are inviting you to give them an answer using a modal verb back, but there are no questions that the examiner asks you to give them an idiom. You have to <u>create the opportunity to use idioms</u>. You have to be confident enough in your English, quick enough with your vocabulary to be able to use idioms properly.

Use idiomatic expressions and phrasal verbs for accurate collocations. The best way to learn phrases is **reading**. Reading will help you learn idiomatic expressions and phrasal verbs for accurate collocations effectively. Reading will help you improve your writing score, listening score, and even your speaking score. These are things that you need to be aware of.

I don't expect you to learn all of English idioms. I only expect you to learn a handle of them (5-6-7-8 idioms) that you know perfectly; that you think you are able to use them perfectly in the exam.

The use of idioms is a high-level skill. Using them properly, not overusing them.

Try to paraphrase as much as you can and use idioms in your speaking. Use fluency markers that you talk about.

You can boost your vocabulary by using paraphrasing, using idioms and you can improve your pronunciation. You can get up to 7.0+ with your pronunciation in 3 months if you practice your pronunciation every day.

<u>LIST OF USEFUL IDIOMS:</u>

It's as easy as pie = it's a piece of cake: to be very easy, (not complicated).

- *I don't think <u>it's as easy as pie</u> to get band 8.5 in the IELTS speaking test.*

- *<u>It's a piece of cake</u> to drive this car.*

Cost an arm and a leg: to be very expensive.

- *The movie is interesting, but the tickets cost an arm and a leg.*
- *The car cost him an arm and a leg.*

Pay through the nose: to pay too much for something.

- *I usually have to pay through the nose for parking a car if I bring it into the city.*
- *He paid through the nose to get the car fixed.*

Make someone blue = bump someone out: to make someone sad or sick.

- *It made him blue to have to stay home with his wife all day.*
- *He made his girlfriend blue yesterday.*

Freak out: to become very angry or lose control of your mind because of somebody or something.

- *I freaked out when I saw her with another man.*
- *Snakes really freaked me out.*

In the nick of time: just before it's too late/ at the last possible moment.

- *We got to the airport just in the nick of time.*
- *I arrived at the train station in the nick of time.*
- *She finished her English essay just in the nick of time.*

It's raining cats and dogs: it's raining a lot/ it is raining heavily.

- *It's windy and is raining cats and dogs.*
- *It was raining cats and dogs, so all flights were delayed.*

(Like) two peas in a pod: very similar, especially in appearance.

- *Peter and his brother are like two peas in a pod.*
- *The twins are like two peas in a pod.*

(As) sly as a fox: someone who is clever, cunning, wily, and tricky.

- *Many people don't like him because he is sly as a fox.*
- *My boss is as sly as a fox.*

Poke around: look around a place, typically in search of something (you can poke around on the internet, you can poke around on the streets, etc. to look for/search for something).

- *Just poke around the Internet, you'll find a lot of dating websites.*
- *He poked around in his desk to see if the wallet was there.*

Mean business: to be very, very serious.

- *I thought he was joking at first, but then I saw that he really meant business.*
- *Just looking at him, I knew he meant business.*

Hit the hay = hit the sack: to go to bed.

- *I'm pretty tired. I think it's time for me to hit the hay.*
- *I'm going to hit the sack early since I've got to get up early tomorrow.*

Sleep like a baby: to sleep very well; to sleep deeply.

- *After a long, hard day at work, I slept like a baby last night.*
- *He was very tired, so he went to bed, and slept like a baby.*

Once in a blue moon: very rarely/very seldom/almost never.

- *My son lives in Canada and he only comes to see us once in a blue moon.*
- *My family used to live in Tokyo, but now we only go there once in a blue moon.*

Ace a test: to do very well in a test/ to get a very high score on a test.

- *You need to study hard to ace a test.*
- *She had actually aced a test in Math, a subject that had never come easily for her.*

Ring a bell: to sound familiar.

- *The name Lucy doesn't ring a bell.*
- *I've never met Sarah, but her name rings a bell.*

Green with envy: to be jealous/ to be envious.

- *Tom was green with envy when he saw that I got a new car for my birthday.*
- *My expensive house makes him green with envy.*

Drive someone crazy: to make him or her upset or annoyed.

- *Tom quit his job because his boss drove him crazy every time he went to work.*
- *The constant noise drove me crazy.*

The cat that ate the canary: to look very happy/ very pleased.

- *He was smiling like the cat that ate the canary.*
- *You look like the cat that ate the canary.*

3. GRAMMAR:

Pay attention to a grammatical range of accuracy.

- *Are you making mistakes?*
- *How many mistakes are you making?*
- *Are those mistakes reducing the examiner's ability to be able to understand you?*

That's the key.

Forget about being perfect, you're not going to be perfect. Don't chase perfection, you never get it. So, what can you do? Well, I would say that you should focus on the big mistakes that you are making usually. Those are verb tenses, article and adjectives like *"I felt so bored* (not boring). Something like that.

Another thing you need to pay your attention to is that subject-verb agreement.

My father has (not have) a motorbike.

4. PRONUNCIATION

Pronunciation is probably the thing you use the most. The fact about pronunciation is that a lot of you need to know how badly it destroys your band score even though your grammar and vocabulary are good. It really does. It kills. So you need to spend time practicing your pronunciation. Pronunciation is by far the easiest thing for you to fix in your English.

Note that pronunciation is 100% physical.

What is a word?

A word is a collection of sounds. For example, the word "MIXED" is a collection of the sounds "M.I.K.S.T"

The problem is that you don't know where the sounds are, you don't know how to make the sounds and you don't do it enough. So try to **practice** your pronunciation enough.

How to be good at pronunciation?

One of the reasons my pronunciation is so clear is that I have focused years for years on finishing my sounds (like, because). My pronunciation is not accidentally clear, my pronunciation is clear by being designed because I am extremely precise with every sound that I have made. You can learn the same thing. It's not magic, it's not intelligent, it's just focused, focused and focused. You have to be precise, and you have to practice pronunciation often.

Work at it every day. Don't try to pronounce the words too fast.

PART 1 SPEAKING ESSENTIALS

What does the word **"essential"** mean? It means *"very important, highly critical, necessary"*

The skills that you learn for part 1 speaking are 100% the foundation of part 2 and part 3 speaking. If you do a poor job in part 1 speaking, the examiner will be supposed to give you just a 5.0 before you have done part 2 & part 3 speaking.

When it comes to part 1 speaking, I would say that you need to remember these things:

<u>Number 1:</u> **Never** answer with <u>only one word</u>. Always use <u>complete sentences</u> or <u>phrases</u>.

If they ask you *"do you like to read?"*

If you just say: **yes**

Well, your answer has no grammar, no pronunciation, no vocabulary. All they know is *"you like to read"*.

What is the better answer of *"do you like to read?"*

<u>Answer:</u> **Yes, I would love to...**

Or: **no, reading is boring. I think that people who read are quite stupid. Frankly, I think they should be doing more fun things like motorbike racing or knife fighting...**

This answer is **better**. You might disagree because the answer sounds a bit rude, and it talks a lot about a bad lifestyle (motorbike racing, knife fighting). However, the examiner is not going to give you a band score based on how nice a person you are, they will give you a band score based on your English ability. So be sure that you give them what they want.

<u>Number 2:</u> you need to show the examiner something or some things

about your English, and that can be something about your grammar, something about your vocabulary, something about the organization of your answer, and maybe something about your pronunciation.

For example, if they ask you *"do you like watching TV?"*

And you say: *of course, I love watching TV.*

When you say *"I love..."* you <u>stressed the word</u> **"love"**. That means you've shown something about your pronunciation.

These are things you need to think about: <u>answer the question</u> and <u>extend your answer</u>. Show something about your English ability. For each question, try to produce your answer in different ways to show different things about your speaking. There are some basic things you can do right away. First of all, you add details by using those basic questions in English: *"who", "what", "when", "where", "why", "how", "how often", "how much", etc.*

So if they ask you *"do you like watching TV?"*

You can say: *Yes, I love watching TV. I really love Mr. Bean. He is my favorite TV character. I often watch TV with my family in the living room on the weekend.*

Or if they ask you *"do you like reading books?"*

You can say: *yes, I really love reading books mainly because it's so relaxing. I remember when I was in high school, my teacher gave me a really good book and inspired me to read more and more.*

Before answering the question, make sure you pay attention to the question type, the verb tense *("<u>do</u> you like to read?"* or *"<u>did</u> you like to read when you <u>were</u> a child?" Or "what book <u>would</u> you <u>like</u> to read?")*. Be careful about this.

<u>For example</u>: *"Do you like reading books?"*

What's the verb tense of this question? *Present tense.*

<u>Answer</u>: *Yes, I really love reading books mainly because it's so relaxing. I remember <u>when I was</u> in high school, my teacher <u>gave</u> me a really good book and <u>inspired</u> me to read more and more.*

Did I answer the question?

Yes, and then I switched from present tense to past tense. That is something else you can do. You can do a lot of things when it comes to extending your answer; you can use non-defining relative clauses to add extra information about anything you want to say. So think about this.

I can say *"I really enjoy reading comic books. These books are very entertaining."* (2 sentences)

But I can combine them and make 1 sentence by using a *non-defining relative clause*.

"I really love reading comic books, which are very entertaining."

Like I said, you can change the verb tense.

If they ask you *"did you enjoy reading books when you were a child?"*

What's the verb tense of this question? *Past tense*, right?

So, be sure you answer the question, but go ahead and switch the verb tense if you want.

You can say: *To be honest, I didn't really like reading so much when I was a kid. But nowadays, I'm pretty keen on reading mystery novels. Actually, I'm going to the bookstore after the class tonight, and I'll buy some mystery novels.*

So I just gave the examiner the answer using past tense, present tense and future tense.

You can use *the adverbs of frequency*. You can talk about *how often* or *how rarely* you do something. Use a range adverbs of frequency and be careful not just giving the adverb back to the examiner.

For example, if they ask you *"what do you usually do on the weekend?"*

You shouldn't say: *on the weekend, I usually*.

That's fine, proper grammar, but if you want to get a high score, you should change *"usually"* into *"frequently"* or *"often"*. You should paraphrase it.

Stay away from using 100% and 0% statement like *always, never*, etc.

Example 1: *"What do you do on the weekend?"*

Answer: *I ~~always~~ go to the mall and talk to everyone*

"Always go to the mall?" does this sound like accurate communication? *Is it possible to always go the mall every weekend?* That sounds a little **strange**.

Example 2: *"What do you do on the weekend?"*

Answer: *I ~~always~~ do my homework.*

Never have a weekend off? Always to 100% of the time on the weekend you do your homework? That doesn't sound like accurate.

Example 3: *"do you like fast food?"*

Answer: *To be honest, it's disgusting, I ~~never~~ eat it.*

Never eat fast food? That doesn't sound like accurate.

So I would say that you should be very careful of using these adverbs of frequency **always** and **never** in your answers.

Paraphrasing: you can use synonyms and parallel expressions to paraphrase the question in your answer.

For example, if they ask you *"what did you like to read as a child?"*

It's very easy to get into the bad habit if you say *"As a child, I ~~like to read~~."*

Your grammar is ok, however, your vocabulary score is low because you didn't show the examiner your vocabulary, you borrowed his vocabulary, and you used it in your answer.

So if they ask you *"what did you like to read as a child?"*

You should paraphrase your answer like *"when I was a kid, I love reading…"* it's much better.

Or you can say *"back then, I enjoyed reading…"*

"Back then" in this case means *"when I was a child"*

Or you can <u>paraphrase your answer</u> by saying: *Yes, I <u>love</u> it. In fact, I <u>have enjoyed reading</u>. I <u>have been reading</u> mystery novels when I <u>was</u> a teenager.* (I used present, present perfect, present perfect continuous in my answer).

Let me give you another example here.

If they ask you *"what do you do in your free time?"*

You should <u>paraphrase your answer</u> by saying: *"In my leisure time/ in my spare time, I love to play games…"*

Or you can say *"when I am not working, I like to read books."*

Or you can say *"well, one of my hobbies is fishing."*

Paraphrasing statements about <u>favorite things/people</u>

If they ask you *"What's your favorite food to eat?"*

If you answer like this *"My favorite food definitely is X because…"*, you <u>will not get a high score</u> because you don't paraphrase.

Instead, you can use this structure ==*"The X I love the most is…"*== to answer this question *"what's your favorite X…?"*

<u>Example:</u> *what's your favorite TV show?*

You can say: *The TV show I love the most is…*

What is your favorite place to visit?

You can say: *The city I love the most is New York…*

So you need to practice this structure, because if the examiner gives you a **"favorite"** question, then you know how to answer it excellently.

On the other hand, if they ask you *"What's your least favorite food to eat?*

You would say: ==*The X I love the least is…*== or ==*I really dislike…*==

"What's your least favorite food to eat?

You can say: *Well, the food I love the least is Kimchi, I generally don't like Korean food....*

Synonyms for Like and Dislike to paraphrase the questions:

LIKE:

Like, to be keen on, to be fond of, to be captivated by, to be fascinated by, to be tempted by, fancy, to be attracted to, to be passionate about.

DISLIKE:

Dislike, to be not keen on, to be not fond of, detest, hate, loathe, can't stand, can't bear, to be not captivated by.

Summary: You will not get a high score (7.0+) if you don't paraphrase your answer. You have to do it. You might be going to be slow at first. I know this, but the more you practice your paraphrasing, the easier it will get. You will be programmed like a computer.

Comparison: You can answer the question by using **comparison language**. Comparison language is so useful. This is something the examiner is expecting you to be able to do. They want you to be able to compare things. **What to compare?** Compare what you want, many things you can compare.

Do you like to read? Compare what you like to read with what you don't like to read. Compare what you like to read now with what you used to like to read when you were a child.

Compare what you like to read now with what you would like to read in the future.

Compare what you like to read with what your friends/your parents/people in your country like to read.

If the examiner gives you a question with one to two choices. They are inviting you to do something, they are hoping that you will be giving them a certain kind of language.

- *Would you rather own a dog or a cat as a pet?*

- *Do you prefer reading books or magazines?*
- *Do you like eating fast food or traditional food?*

First of all, you are going to <u>PARAPHRASE</u>. If they ask you *"Would you rather...?"*, you are going to answer *"I would prefer to..."*

<u>Example:</u> *Would you rather own a dog or a cat as a pet?*

Your answer should be *"I <u>would prefer to</u> own a dog/ I <u>would prefer to</u> own a cat."*

If they ask you *"Would you prefer to own a dog or a cat as a pet?"*

Your answer should be *"I <u>would rather</u> own a dog/ I <u>would rather</u> own a cat."*

Always note that comparison language is the thing that the examiner really wants you to do in your speaking. I promise to you that if you want to get a high score in the exam, you need to be able to compare. They want you to be able to *<u>compare</u>*. Also, they need you to use *<u>non-defining relative clauses</u>*, *<u>dependent clauses</u>*, and make sure that each sentence should have a purpose.

If this, then...however if this, then...

Given the option, I would prefer to...

My preference would be.....

PRACTICE:

Would you rather go to the movie or sing karaoke on Friday night?

STEP 1: You can start your answer by saying something that is <u>generally true about both things.</u>

- *Well, <u>both of them are</u> fun activities.*
- *Well, <u>both of them are</u> things that I really like to do.*
- *Well, <u>both of those activities are</u> things that my friends and I really love.*

STEP 2: Then you can start <u>describing more details</u> (positive and negative) about the two things <u>using comparison structures</u>:

Would you rather own a dog or a cat as a pet?

Both of them are really fun. However (now you start talking about one of them) dogs have <u>more personality</u> and are very loyal (positive). But, they can <u>require more time</u> and a bigger home to take care of them properly (negative). Cats, on the other hand do not need <u>as much space as</u> dogs (positive). Also, they are <u>much more independent</u> (positive). However, they can be <u>less friendly than</u> dogs (negative).

STEP 3: Making your choice:

Given the option (what I am doing here is signaling that <u>I am making my choice</u>) I <u>would prefer</u> to have a dog because they are easier to have a strong relationship with.

Adjectives: you can use adjectives in your answer to describe things or people. Be sure to use adjectives with proper forms **"V-ED"** or **"V-ING"** exactly.

V-ED adjective: is used for the person or the thing <u>doing a feeling</u>.

V-ING adjective: is used for the thing <u>causing the feeling</u>.

- <u>Example 1</u>: You are at the theater. When you are watching the movie, someone who is sitting next to you is talking. They are *annoying*. That's why you feel *annoyed*.

- <u>Example 2</u>: When you go to the beach. The beach is so *relaxing*. That's why you feel so *relaxed*.

- <u>Example 3</u>: I was very *excited* because the movie was so *exciting*.

- <u>Example 4</u>: I wasn't *bored* because the movie was so *exciting*.

Remember to explain your adjectives. <u>Don't leave</u> these adjectives <u>unclear</u>. You should explain them by answering the question **"why?"** and <u>giving examples</u>.

Why A better than B?

Why was the movie so interesting?

Relative Clauses/ Relative Pronouns: you can use relative clauses or relative pronouns and past participle to add specific details in your answer. For example:

"I really like jumping into the river. This is a lot of fun." **"This"** is a relative pronoun.

You can make this sentence by using a relative clause *"I really like jumping into the river, which is a lot of fun."*

- I like people *who give me money.*
- I like activities *that are healthy.*
- I really like people *who give me money.*
- *These people* are very friendly and I love them.
- Of all his friends, I am the one *who* he knows he can rely on.

Try to give extra information by using relative clauses extremely flexible. We use relative clauses for part 1, part 2, part 3 speaking and even for task 1 and task 2 writing.

Number 3: Is the question about you or the question about other people?

If the examiner asks you *"do you like to read?"* or *"do you enjoy shopping?"* they are asking about you.

If the examiner asks you *"why do people enjoy reading?"* or *"why do people enjoy shopping?"*, they are not asking about you, they are asking about the people in general.

Be sure if they ask you *"do you like to read?"*

Again, you **shouldn't** say like this: *yes, reading is very popular, a lot of people like to read because it's so relaxing and helps them build their knowledge, so people read in their free time quite a lot....*

How is the grammar in the answer? The grammar is great. How is the vocabulary? The vocabulary is great. Unfortunately, I don't know if you don't understand the question or if you don't have the ability to answer in a proper way because you lack English skills. The examiner asked the question about you, and you answered the question about people in general. That's a problem. Be sure you got it.

Number 4: Is the question open or closed?

+ **Closed questions** are the ones that you can answer with *"yes"* or *"no"* or *"it depends"*

Example: *Do you enjoy watching television?*

+ **Open question** are the ones that you do not answer with *"yes"* or *"no"* or *"it depends"*

Example: *Why do people like watching television?*

This is a big difference because if they ask you about a closed question, you will give **a yes/no answer**.

Number 5: **Start and end your answer with confidence:** answer the question, show something or some things about your English ability and stop talking and let them ask you another question. Do not make your part 1 speaking answers too long. Don't do it, the examiner will get frustrated. They have questions that are designed to get different responses from you.

If they ask you *"do you like to read?"*

Don't answer the question too long like this *"yes, I love reading and I really enjoy reading mystery novels. A lot of people don't like mystery novels, but I really love them. When I was a child, I really loved reading comic books; back then I really love to read bad man."*

So please well prepare and focus on how to answer different types of IELTS questions. Plan and practice ways to answer questions clearly and fluently. Be specific about what you are studying, focus on something and practice regularly. Then, in the exam, be disciplined and stick with your plan. Know what you want to say and how you want to say it. Then you will easily get a high score in your part 1 speaking.

Number 7: **Develop good habits.** You should study many times a week, but only for 5-10 minutes for each time. Research has proved that this is the best way to master vocabulary and phrases. Try to avoid long study sessions only once a week. Practice whenever you have some free time, set small goals, and, if you do this regularly, you will make great improvements.

Number 8: There are some essential topics you must be prepared to discuss: your favorites (food, books, films, TV shows, personal item, website, etc.)...people in your life (family, friends, teachers, neighbors)...activities (hobbies, exercise, what you do on holidays, memories of past and plans for future), places (where you live, where you might like to live, places to visit, etc), and things (devices and gadgets you use every day, presents you have given or received, valuable and cherished objects).

Number 9: **Relax and be natural.**

FLUENCY MARKERS

What are fluency markers (discourse markers)?

Fluency markers are words or phrases that native speakers use to make their speaking sound more natural, smoother and clearer. We use these words or phrases to signal information.

You will not get a high score in the speaking test, part 1, part 2, or part 3 if you don't learn how to signal your answers, how to combine and link your sentences together. What you are seeing below are great examples that involve the fluency markers using different time expressions as well as different verb forms. I don't just use past simple, I use past continuous, and present perfect that we will need to do in the speaking test.

One of the fluency markers we've already talked about is **"however"**. When you hear *"however"*, you know that will be signaling, changing about something.

For example: *Vietnam is really hot, and sometimes it rains which is very convenient.* ***However***…(now what I am saying about Vietnam, something positive or something negative?)

Something positive because you know when we are saying something…***however***…we will be signaling or we will be talking about something different.

My friends really love to go to the movie on Friday night. ***However,***…(I could be talking something they don't like to do like *"My friends really love to go to the movie on Friday night. However, they hate singing karaoke."*

So we can use these words to signal a lot of information. Practice using these fluency markers, then it will become your habit.

Let's talk about other fluency markers.

1. To be honest/ I'm afraid/ honestly: these are what we call softening phrases. We use these phrases to be more polite when we get a negative answer, or to signal that we are going to give a negative answer or you are not proud of what you will say.

Examples: *Do you enjoy reading?*

- *To be honest*, I don't really like reading.
- *Honestly*, I don't like reading very much.
- *I'm afraid*, I don't like it very much.

You are Japanese. How do you feel if you ask someone *"do you like Japanese food?"* and they say *"I don't like it"* Does that sound a bit rude? Yes, it sounds quite harsh. So you need to be more gentle with your negative answers or when you are not proud of something.

So it will sound better if you say *"honestly, I don't like Japanese food very much"*

However, what if I ask you *"do you smoke cigarettes?"*

Can you say *"To be honest, I don't smoke"*. Is it something you should feel ashamed of? **No**, you should be proud that you are not a smoker. Something like that, even though the answer is no, you don't really need to get the fluency marker *"To be honest/ I'm afraid/ honestly"* in this case.

2. Fortunately/ unfortunately: these are really great and easy-to-use words that students don't practice enough. They don't use them enough. These words are powerful and easy. We use these words to signal a positive or negative situation or condition, and we can use them in a combination. You can talk about the negative, and then, fortunately, a positive; or a positive, unfortunately, a negative.

<u>Example 1:</u> I remember it rained heavily that day (a negative). **Fortunately**, I had my umbrella with me (a positive).

<u>Example 2:</u> My mother cooks for me every day (a positive). **Unfortunately**, she's not a very good cook (a negative).

So, we can use these things in a combination.

You should practice using fluency markers in a combination with one another.

Example 3: *Do you enjoy reading?*

To be honest, *I'm not really keen on reading books.* **Unfortunately**, *I'm in university and my professor requires a lot of reading.*

So I just answer the question and I use two fluency markers. It's really helpful to make your speaking become more organized.

3. Actually/ In fact /As a matter of fact: We use these words to add details.

Example: *Do you enjoy reading?*

To be honest, I don't like to read very much. Unfortunately, I'm in university right now, and my professor gives me a lot of reading assignments. In fact, tonight I will have to read about 40 pages…

Ok. That works. Again, you should use all these fluency markers in a combination because that will help you get a better speaking score.

Actually: This can be used as a softening phrase. If I ask my girlfriend *"baby, do you love me?"* she says *"actually, you are not handsome, so I don't love you."*

4. However/ but: these words are used to signal a different idea or opinion. That could be a difference between now and in the past; or a difference between now and the future.

Example 1: *Do you enjoy traveling?*

Well, I love traveling. Unfortunately, I'm quite busy right now, so I haven't had a chance to go anywhere, **but** *I'm planning to travel to Thailand during Tet holiday.*

Example 2: *Going to the beach is a lot of fun.* **However**, *I would rather explore a big city.*

5. I suppose /I guess: These words are used to indicate a speculation. Speculation basically means *a guess.*

When you answer the question by using phrases *"I suppose or I guess"*, what you are showing the listener is that you do not know the exact answer, but you are <u>trying very hard to give the best guess</u>.

Example 1: *What's the population of Ho Chi Minh City?*

You can say something like: *that's a good question, I really don't know, but **I guess/suppose** it's about ten million people.*

Example 2: *What's the best university in the United States?*

You can say something like: *I **suppose** it's the Harvard University.*

6. Supposedly/ supposed to be: These words are called <u>stereotype language</u>.

What is a **stereotype**?

A stereotype is something that you <u>have heard is true</u>, but you <u>do not know</u> because you <u>have not experienced it</u>.

Example: *There are a lot of guns, violence in America.*

If you have never been to America, you **should not** say *"America is a violent country"* because you have never been there. Instead, you should say: *America <u>is supposed to be</u> a very violent country.*

Or: <u>*some people say that*</u> *living in New York is very enjoyable.*

7. I've heard (that) / some people say (that)

Use to express what you <u>have heard to be true</u>, but do not know by yourself, because you <u>have not experienced it</u>.

Vietnamese food is supposed to be delicious. <u>I've heard (that)</u> Vietnamese food is delicious.

TIME AND FREQUENCY EXPRESSIONS

1. Nowadays/ these days: We use these words for <u>current actions and habits</u>.

<u>Example:</u> *Do you enjoy watching television?*

Yes, I love watching television. Unfortunately, I don't have a lot of free time. <u>Nowadays</u>, I am doing a lot of studying at the university and I don't have a chance to watch my favorite programs.

Or: ……<u>Nowadays</u>, I often watch cartoons. I especially like Tom & Jerry.

2. Used to + Verb: We use this structure to talk about <u>past actions and habits</u>.

- *I <u>used to</u> go swimming with my friends.*
- *I <u>used to</u> yell at my coworkers.*

3. When I was X: we use this structure to talk about <u>past actions and habits</u>.

- *<u>When I was a university student</u>, I used to meet my friends for coffee every morning before class.*
- *I used to go to the library <u>when I was in high school</u>.*
- *I used to cook for my brother <u>when I was a teenager</u>.*

4. Adverbs of Frequency: We use adverbs of frequency *Never… Seldom/ rarely/ hardly ever… Sometimes… Often/ Frequently/ Nearly always …Usually/ typically/ normally… Always* to tell <u>how often something is done</u>

- *I <u>never</u> feel bored when I talk with him.*
- *I <u>seldom/ rarely/ hardly ever</u> go swimming on Sunday morning.*

- I *often* go to the university canteen to eat with my friends.

- I *usually* go to bed by 11 p.m.

5. Adverbs of Infrequency: *Every once in a while / Every so often / Every now and then / Every now and again.* Use in place of "sometimes and seldom"

- *Every once in a while* I play sports on the weekend.

- I play golf *every so often*.

- *Every now and then* we stay in bed all day and watch cartoons.

6. Concession and contrast: something is true; however, something else is true. We use this a lot. This is a massively useful structure because we use this structure a lot for part 1, part 2, part 3 speaking and task 2 writing.

Is watching TV popular in your country?

Teenagers and little children really enjoy watching television. However, the elderly prefer reading the newspaper.

Do you like food from other countries?

Well, food from other places is very delicious. However, I prefer eating food from Vietnam.

ADVERBIALS FOR GIVING OPINIONS

1. Personally: you are only giving your own opinion about something.

Personally, I don't think organized social events are very important.

2. Frankly/to be frank: you are saying something direct and honest.

Frankly/ to be frank, I don't like Korean food.

3. Typically: this situation is usually true or this is what usually happens.

4. Obviously/ clearly: a fact can be easily noticed or understood.

Obviously, the first aim of primary education is to teach students basic literacy skills.

5. Predictably/ inevitably: this situation was expected or certain to happen.

Predictably, most people find exams are stressful.

6. Inevitably/surprisingly: this situation was unexpected.

Surprisingly, ability is usually judged by exam results.

QUESTIONS ABOUT OTHER PEOPLE:

Quantities of people: *nearly everyone, almost everybody, the (vast) majority of + types of people, most + types of people, a large percentage of + types of people, some + types of people, a few + types of people, a handful of + types of people.*

Phrases of habit (showing that you are talking about a group): *as a rule, tend to, generally speaking.*

Types of people - ages: *young adults, people who are older, students, people who love animals,*

Types of people - behavior: *energetic people, sad people/ people who are sad, people with a sense of humor, lazy people, sporty people, religious people...*

Adjectives of evaluation (what we think about something): *thrilling, relaxing, interesting, fascinating, stimulating, exciting, inspiring, etc.*

USEFUL STRUCTURES:

S + believe/find something + Adjective

- They <u>find</u> comic books <u>boring</u>.

- I <u>find</u> it <u>exciting/wonderful</u>.

- I <u>find</u> it <u>delicious</u>.

- As a rule, most teenage boys <u>find</u> videos games <u>very exciting</u>.

Is watching cartoon a popular hobby in your country?

Yes, most children tend to watch animation. They are really keen on Tom & Jerry. Personally, I don't really like these shows. I find them a bit boring.

Why do some people enjoy horror films?

- Who enjoys horror films?

- Why do they enjoy horror films?

Using <u>adjectives</u> and <u>explanations for adjectives</u>: ....*they <u>find</u> horror films really <u>thrilling</u>. However, not many elderly like this genre because they tend to <u>find</u> them really <u>disgusting</u>.*

Do people in your country enjoy fast food?

- Who enjoys fast food? (Teenagers, young adults)

- Why do they enjoy fast food?

HIGH-SCORE VOCABULARY

Instead of saying *"I was very afraid"*, you can say *"I was <u>terrified</u>"*. It's much better when it comes to vocabulary.

Instead of saying *"my neighbor's cat is very big"*, you can say *"my neighbor's cat is immense"*

Instead of saying *"his car is very fast"*, you can say *"his car is speedy"*.

PART 1 SPEAKING PRACTICE

QUESTIONS ABOUT WHERE YOU ARE LIVING

What kind of town or city are you living in at the moment?

You might say: *I live in a residential area in a highly populated city.*

<u>Extend your answer:</u> *I live in a big city. Actually, I live in a south side of Ho Chi Minh City. It's a residential area near a busy intersection.* (Try to focus on <u>*place language*</u>, and <u>*prepositions*</u>, then you will get a high score.)

How long do you live here? *I <u>have lived</u> here/I <u>have been living</u> here for about 5 years* (present perfect or present perfect continuous).

Or you can use the structure "since"

- *I have lived here/I have been living here <u>since</u> I started university.*

- *I have lived here/I have been living here <u>since</u> I began my job 2 years ago.*

QUESTIONS ABOUT ENTERTAINMENT: You can say something like *go shopping, drink coffee, singing karaoke, play sports, etc.*

You need to use a verb. You can <u>talk about what you do</u>, and you can <u>talk about what other people do</u>. That's is a great opportunity for you to show your vocabulary.

You can answer: *As a rule, young people in my neighborhood.../ As a rule, <u>the young people</u> where I live usually sing karaoke, drink a lot of beer, and ride a motorbike. However, <u>the elderly</u> tend to prefer to watch horror films.*

How would you describe the people who live there? (Using adjectives)

They are <u>nice</u>, <u>friendly</u>, <u>supportive</u>...

What you like most about living there? (Using superlatives)

- *The thing I love the most is…*

- *My favorite thing about Sydney is…*

- *I really love…*

- *What I really love is…*

What is your least favorite thing? (Using superlatives)

- *The thing I dislike the most is….*

- *Well, I really hate…*

- *The thing I really hate is…*

ADJECTIVES THAT ARE USED TO DESCRIBE PLACES:

- *Wild = remote*

- *My home is in the middle of nowhere (idiom) = very rural.*

- *It's off the beaten track: a place where people don't normally go/ a place is remote/ unusual area.*

- *Exciting = vibrant*

- *Friendly place = welcoming place = hospitable place*

- *A busy area = a crowded/ bustling/ hustle and bustle urban area.*

- *A dull place = not a very exciting place = a boring place*

- *A deserted place = an empty place (nobody around)*

- *Relaxing place = the place is very relaxing.*

QUESTIONS ABOUT MUSIC:

What type of music do you like most?

You might say: *My favorite style is jazz (**don't repeat** the word "music" by saying*

~~my favorite type of music is~~) *mainly because it's so relaxing after a stressful day at work.*

Or: *I am* <u>*a huge fan of jazz*</u>*. Actually, I will drive* (simple future) *to a club tonight (when) to listen to (why) a famous jazz guitarist (who).*

Or: *I am* <u>*a huge fan of jazz*</u>*. Actually, I will be driving* (future continuous) *to a club tonight (when) to listen to (why) a famous jazz guitarist (who).*

We use future continuous to talk about something <u>in progress at a certain time</u>. With future continuous, you <u>need a time in the future</u>.

Next year I <u>*will be studying*</u> *in London.*

Two weeks from now, I <u>*will be flying*</u> *home for Tet holiday.*

We use future perfect to talk about <u>a completed action in the future</u>.

Luckily, by the end of the summer, my favorite band <u>*will have played*</u>*.*

I am <u>*a huge fan of*</u> *Vietnamese food.*

We can use various verb tenses in the answer: *Last night, I* <u>*fell asleep*</u> *(paste tense) while I* <u>*was listening*</u> *(paste continuous) to music on my ear phones* (two verb forms in one sentence)

How often did you play sports when you were young?

Back then, I used to meet my friends (who) for football matches (why) a few times a month (how often).

What do you do on the weekend?

Answer 1: *My favorite type of music is Jazz. In fact, I love playing guitar (what) with my friends (who) in my bedroom (where) on the weekends (when). Sadly, I'm terrible (how), but I find it relaxing (why) (why I play guitar).*

Answer 2: *In fact, my father who shares his collection of music with me (what) when I was a teen (when). I love sitting in the living room (where) and relaxing while listening to his collection on my headphone (how).*

Answer 3: *Honestly,* <u>*my friends are very keen on*</u> *playing sports* <u>*but I prefer to*</u> *play guitars*

Do people in your country enjoy eating fast food?

Note: This is a question not about you, it's about other people.

Answer 1: *Yes, many of them do, especially teens. They are fans of cheese burger....*

Answer 2: *It depends, many Vietnamese teens like cheese burgers, but not a lot of them like KFC (something they do, something they don't).*

PREFERENCE QUESTIONS

What are preference questions?

Preference questions always give you choice *(would you rather do this or would you rather do that? do you prefer to do this or do you prefer to do that? do you like to do this or do you like to do that?)*

Example: *Would you rather see a romantic film or comedy?*

As a rule, with these questions, the examiner wants you to talk about both things. They are signaling to you that if they give you those types of question, they want you to talk about both things, they want you to compare by using comparison structures. You should do a couple of things here:

Would you rather own a dog or a cat as a pet?

STEP 1: You can start your answer by saying something that is generally true about both things.

Well, both of them are really fun.

STEP 2: Then you can start describing more details (positive and negative) about the two things using comparison structures:

However (now you start talking about one of them) dogs have more personality and are very loyal (positive). But, they can require more time and a bigger home to take care of them properly (negative). Cats, on the other hand, do not need as much space as dogs (positive). Also, they are much more independent (positive). However, they can be less friendly than dogs (negative).

STEP 3: Making your choice:

Given the option (what I am doing here is signaling that I am making my choice) I would prefer to have a dog because they are easier to have a strong relationship with.

Note: in order to get a high score in the speaking test, you have to paraphrase the question.

If they say *"would you rather eat bananas or apples?"*

You should say: *I'd prefer to eat apples* or *I'd prefer to eat bananas.*

If they say *"would you rather"*, you should say *"I would prefer"*

If they ask you *"would you prefer to eat bananas or apples?"*

You should say *"I would rather eat apples"*

PART 1 SPEAKING MODEL ANSWERS

"WORK" TOPIC

Do you work or are you a student?

Answer: *I am studying and working at the same time. Before I came to France, I was working as an engineer, but at the moment I'm studying French because I hope to do a Master's here.*

Do you like your job?

Answer: *well, generally speaking, I really enjoy my job simply because it's very rewarding to be able to help people every day. It also helps me boost my people skills, expand my social network and give me a financial security.*

Do you like your study?

Answer: *Yes, I really love studying law, but my real aim is to do a Master's and then look for a job in an international law firm.*

What do you like about your job?

Answer: *Frankly, I love everything about my current job. But, I think the best part of it is that I could travel and discover places that I have never been to.*

Is there anything you don't like about your job?

Answer: *Generally speaking, I enjoy my job. The only thing I am not so fond of is the salary; it's not good enough for me to enjoy my life. I wish my boss would give me a pay rise next month.*

Would you like to change your job in the future?

Answer: *I don't want to get stuck at the job that I am working now. I am still young, so 1 want to learn as much as I can. Moreover, I would like to be my own boss, so I'm planning to run my own business next year.*

"HOME TOWN" TOPIC

Where are you from? Where is your hometown?

Answer: *I'm from Ho Chi Minh, which is a city in the south of Vietnam.*

Do you like your home town? (Why?)

Answer: *Yes, I like living in Ho Chi Minh City mainly because it's where most of my friends and family members live, and because there are a lot of activities to do here. The only thing I don't like is the traffic; it's nearly always crowded and noisy.*

Would you prefer to live somewhere else? (Why?)

Answer: *For now, I'm happy living here. But at some point when I get old, I'd probably like to live in a place with a warmer climate, and many beautiful natural landscapes including beaches.*

Is your hometown suitable for young people to live in?

Answer: *Definitely yes, Ho Chi Minh City is a perfect place for young people to live in simply because it has lots of things for young generation to enjoy, such as sports facilities, gyms, schools, hospitals, public transport, and even leisure facilities.*

MUSIC TOPIC

Do you like music?

Answer: *Definitely yes. Music is my cup of tea. I love pop, hip hop, rock, and classical music mainly because it can cheer me up greatly when I feel bored or tired. I usually listen to music from my earphones when I'm traveling from place to place.*

Somebody's cup of tea: means what somebody likes or is interested in.

How often do you usually listen to music?

Answer: *Almost every day. Normally, I listen to music whenever I feel bored or depressed. I have favorite different playlists that can help me get into a particular mood whenever I feel down. Also, I like listening to music when I can't go to sleep, I like to listen to some light music to calm myself down.*

What kinds of music do you like?

Answer: *When it comes to music, yes, I am a big fan of all types of films, such as pop,* hip hop, rock, and classical music. I love listening to music simply because it can cheer myself up/ amuse myself/ relax myself/ release my pressure.

"FILM TOPIC"

Do you like watching films?

<u>Answer:</u> *Absolutely yes, I enjoy watching all types of films, such as romance, action, comedy, sci-fi, and cartoon. Normally when I want to relax, or have some fun I am really keen on watching films at cinemas since it has a better atmosphere with better sounds and visual effects.*

What kinds of films do you like best?/ What's your favorite film?

<u>Answer:</u> *Comedies are my favorite kinds of films. I love this genre simply because it can make me laugh and amuse myself when I feel bored.*

How often do you watch films?

<u>Answer:</u> *Normally, I enjoy watching films at cinemas when I am available during weekends. I like to watch a film with my friends so we could share a good time together, and afterward we will talk about the movie, whether we enjoyed it or not.*

Do you prefer to watch films in the cinema or at home?

<u>Answer 1:</u> *I prefer to watch movies at the cinema simply because it offers me an exciting atmosphere with better sound system and visual effects, so I could be more deeply involved in the film.*

<u>Answer 2:</u> *Mostly, I have a fancy for watching films at home simply because I can choose any movie I want to enjoy and I can watch it in my leisure time. Moreover, I can switch it off or switch channels when I feel uninterested. It is so convenient.*

OTHER TOPICS

Do you like dancing?

<u>Answer:</u> *Definitely yes, I am really keen on dancing. After a hard day at work, I often dance in a dance studio/ gym. I love dancing mainly because it is a great way to exercise my body and that keeps my body fit.*

Do you like traveling?

Answer: *Definitely yes, traveling is my most favorite. When I am free from study/when I am off work, I like to travel to different places with family members or my best friends. I love traveling simply because it brings me a lot of benefits. Particularly I can broaden my horizon. For example, I can meet different people from different places, try different food, and even learn different languages and cultures.*

Do You Prefer To Travel Alone Or With Others?

Answer 1: *Well, I definitely would rather travel with a group of friends simply because I would like to share many things, such as accommodation, transport and even laughter with my mates during the trip. It is much more fun and enjoyable. We can discover new things, try different foods, meet different people, and explore different places together. If I travel alone, I suppose I will be lonely and I may be even helpless when I am into trouble. So traveling in a group of friends is my preference.*

Answer 2: *I would prefer to travel alone. If I travel with a group, I may waste a lot time to wait for the entire group to be ready and complete everything. As a result, I will have less time to meet and make friends with different people when we eat and sightsee together. However, when I travel alone, I can plan the trip by myself, I will have more opportunities to discover new places, people and customs by myself. I can spend more time looking for and making friends with either other tourists or locals during my trip. Particularly, I will be able to decide to do whatever I like without depending on others.*

What is your favourite transport?

Answer: *Although there is a variety of transport choices such as buses, taxies, trains, subways, so on, my favorite way to travel is by plane, because it's quick and convenient, it is more punctual than other means of transport.*

How do you like to travel for a long-distance trip?

Answer: *Personally speaking, I would choose airplane as my priority for a long-distance trip simply because then it doesn't take me so long to get to my destination. Obviously, the airplane is the fastest way of transport, and I don't want to waste my valuable time on the trip.*

Do you have a driving license?

Answer: *Yes, I got my driving license since I was 20 years old, and I am planning to buy a new car for my travel next month.*

Do you prefer to be a driver or a passenger?

Answer: *Generally speaking, I would rather be a passenger mainly because it makes me less stressful and nervous. I don't need to pay my attention to the traffic, and I can spend time doing something like reading books or listening to music on my phone.*

What do you usually do on your holiday?

Answer: *I live far away from my parents so whenever it is time for holidays, normally I go back home to have a get-together with my family and best friends to celebrate holidays. Sometimes I prefer to travel to new places to broaden my horizons and enjoy breathtaking views.*

How often do you have holidays?

Answer: *Well, since I am a college student, so normally I enjoy two main periods when holidays last long, which are the summer holiday and Lunar new year holiday.*

Is it important to have holidays?

Answer: *Absolutely yes, holidays are really necessary for us to rest and give us a chance to do whatever we want to. For example, we can travel to different places to recharge our battery, or spend time with our loved ones so we could be revitalized and refreshed for study or work.*

What kind of places do you like to travel to?

Answer: *I love traveling to many places with beautiful natural landscapes and mountains that I've never explored before. However, I don't often have the opportunity to go to places like that due to lack of funds. So instead I would love to go to places where I can enjoy myself and do fun things together with my friends.*

Do you like doing sports?

Answer: *Certainly yes, I am a big fan of all sorts of sport, including football, badminton, jogging, cycling, and swimming. I find sports very beneficial in a variety of ways; for example, playing a sport can help me relax myself, lose weight and build my body. Playing sports is also a great way for me to socialize and strengthen teamwork spirit with my friends.*

Do you like reading?

Answer: *Absolutely yes, reading is really my cup of tea. I love to read all kinds of book including novels, newspapers, magazines, and textbooks. Obviously, reading is a part of my daily life simply because reading can help me broaden my horizon and keep up with the latest news and information.*

Do you read the newspaper?

Answer: *Certainly yes, but I prefer to read news online instead of paper form because it can help save the natural resources. Also, reading news on the website is totally free of charge. I can read news on my smart phone anytime, anywhere. It's very convenient.*

How often do you read books?

Answer: *Honestly, I'm a complete bookworm. I read all the time. I can read up to 20 books a week. I usually read comic books, but sometimes I change my reading habit slightly by reading books about science or nature. I prefer reading comic books simply because they are great way for me to relax myself and escape from my daily life routines, but I also enjoy science and nature books since they help me enrich my knowledge about the world I live in.*

Do you like shopping?

Answer: *Definitely yes, when talking about shopping, I must say that I am a really shopaholic. In my spare time, I like to go shopping at a supermarket for daily necessities, like cosmetics, skin care products, fashion stuff, and foods. I love shopping for a variety of reasons; for example, I can relax myself, meet my requirements on a daily basis and have an opportunity to catch up with the latest trend and fashion.*

Do you like collecting things?

Answer: *Yes, I'm really keen on collecting things. I have been collecting stamps and coins since I was a child, and I find this activity quite interesting. Collecting stamps and coins is very beneficial in a variety of ways for example it can help me acquire the knowledge of the world and cheer me up greatly when I feed bored.*

Is your family important to you?

Answer: *Absolutely yes, my family is the most important thing in my life. My parents gave me life, brought me up, and always supported me whenever I had difficulties. Without my family, I could not survive for more than three days and I don't think my life* would be meaningful. Obviously, my family means everything to me.

Are computers important to you?

Answer: Certainly yes, computers are extremely necessary in my work and my study. Without computers, it would be inconvenient for me to complete my homework, do research online and even amuse myself since I am used to relaxing myself by playing computer games, listening to music, and chatting with my friends on computers every day.

Do you prefer swimming in the sea or in a swimming pool?

Answer: As a matter of fact, I would rather swim in a swimming pool than in the ocean simply because it's much safer, and I can avoid being attacked by a shark.

Do you prefer to travel by bike or by bus?

Answer: I would rather ride bicycle than travel by bus simply because it's so much more comfortable, convenient and even faster if I'm travelling during the rush hours and particularly I won't get stuck in traffic jams. Besides, cycling also provides me a great way to stay healthier as compared to other means of transport, including buses.

Do you prefer eating at home or at restaurant? Do you prefer to eat out or eat at home?

Answer 1: To be honest, I don't know how to cook and don't have someone to cook for me, so I would rather eat at restaurants than eat at home simply because restaurants usually offer me a more comfortable environment to eat and get together with my friends. In addition, I can also try a wider range of food that tastes more delicious than home-cooked meals like sushi, sashimi, and udon noodles. Furthermore, I don't need to worry about washing dishes when I finish eating. So, given the option, eating at restaurant is certainly my ideal choice.

Answer 2: I would rather eat at home simply because this can help enhance our relationships while we are preparing our meals and enjoying food together. What I mean is during our meals, we can talk, tell jokes and exchange feelings on our current affairs with each other so that we who are parents and children would have a chance to communicate with each other to keep track of what we are thinking and doing. In addition, eating at home is much cheaper than eating at restaurants, and certainly helps us save a lot of money. Furthermore, foods cooked at home will be more hygienic and guaranteed. So, given the option, I would prefer to eat at home.

Which Do You Prefer, Saturday Or Sunday?

Answer: *Personally speaking, I prefer Saturday rather than Sunday simply because I have more freedom and I find it more relaxing, and I can do freely what exactly I want to do. To be specific, I can have some drinks and stay out late at night with my friends without worrying about waking up early for work the next morning. In addition, that is also a great opportunity for us to relax, release pressure and strengthen our relationship after a hard week at work.*

Do You Prefer Watching Sports Events On TV Or Live?

Answer: *Personally speaking, I would rather watch sports on TV than attend a live game simply because it is more time-saving, convenient, enjoyable and less costly than watching sports live. To be specific, I can stay home and enjoy my favorite sports on TV without traveling a long distance from my home to the stadium and might face the congestion of the traffic of the stadiums. It's more comfortable and safer. More importantly, I may be able to see the game, the view of the players or the goal situations from all angles due to the close distance. Furthermore, when watching sports events on Tv, I can share my ideas and feelings with my family and friends; we can cheer our team up with a cup of beer, and enjoy our satisfaction and happiness.*

So, given the option, I would prefer to watch sports on TV.

Do You Prefer Reading An Electronic Book Or A Real Book?

Answer: *Personally, I would rather read electronic books mainly because it is more convenient. What I mean is electronic books are portable, easy to manage, and particularly free of charge. I don't have to carry a pile of books in my bag pack. What I need to do is just to turn on my kindle device and then start reading whatever I have in my mobile library.*

Do you prefer shopping online or at a real store?

Answer: *Personally, I would rather shop online simply because it is more convenient. What I mean is shopping online saves me a lot of time as well as money since I tend to have the opportunity to search for specific items with better prices and quality. In addition, I can order things online and get them delivered within the same day.*

Do you prefer relaxing at home or outside?

Answer: *It depends, during the day I would rather be out of the house; therefore, I would like to go shopping or meet up with friends for playing sports or getting something to eat. However, in the evenings I tend to prefer to relax myself at home by surfing the internet or watching action films.*

Do you prefer writing letters or e-mails?

Answer: *Personally, I prefer communication by email simply because it is more economical, easier, cheaper and a lot quicker to communicate rather than writing a letter. For example, I am going to apply for a job at a Korean company overseas; if I sent a letter to the employer, it might take several weeks to arrive, and all my applications might be delayed. Furthermore, writing letters is more convenient since I can write to more than one person at the same time. Also, it's easy to attach photographs and documents to an email.*

All in all, I would rather write emails rather than write letters.

What do you like to do in your spare time?

Answer: *Well, there are a lot of activities I enjoy doing in my leisure time. I love swimming and I'm also quite into cycling. From time to time, I'm keen on reading books and taking photos. However, what I particularly enjoy doing is listening to classical music – it's so relaxing.*

What do you like to do in the evening?

Answer: *During the day I work really hard so in the evening, I would love to relax myself. I enjoy spending time with my family. I'm really keen on watching films, listening to rock music or reading books. From time to time, I prefer to go for a walk in the park with my wife.*

What do you like most about student life?

Answer: *The thing I particularly love about when I was a university student is the golden opportunity it gave me to enrich my knowledge and establish new relationships. To be specific, at university, I can not only increase my knowledge about my major, but I can also make lots of new friends.*

What is the best thing about your hometown?

Answer: *My hometown is Ha Noi, which is the capital city located in the north of*

Vietnam. The best thing I would like to talk about my hometown is its amazing history, architecture, local food and people. Ha Noi is the biggest city in Vietnam that is famous for many beautiful natural landscapes, tourist attractions and friendly people. But what I particularly value about my hometown is its local food. There are various types of food which are very delicious and easy to find out around the city.

LIST OF PART 1 SPEAKING QUESTIONS TO PRACTICE AT HOME

QUESTIONS ABOUT YOU:

1. What do you dislike about X?
2. How often do you do X?
3. What do you like most about X?
4. Do you prefer X to Y?
5. What do you usually/normally do?
6. What do you like to do (in your spare time)?
7. When was the first/last time you did X?
8. Did you ever learn to do X?
9. How would you improve X?
10. What do you want/hope to do (in the future)?

QUESTIONS ABOUT OTHER PEOPLE:

1. How has X changed?
2. How important is X?
3. Do people do/get enough X?
4. How can people find out about X?
5. Is X popular (in your country)?
6. Why do some people like X?
7. Is it difficult to do X?
8. Is X suitable for (types of people)?
9. What is the best time (of year) to do X?
10. Should people be given X?

WORK

1. What's your job?
2. Why did you choose that kind of work?
3. How long have you been doing it?
4. What is a typical day like at your work?

5. Are there things you don't like about it? What are they?

STUDYING

1. What subjects are you studying?
2. Why did you choose those subjects?
3. How long have you been studying them?
4. Do you enjoy them? Why?
5. What is the best thing about studying?

MOVIES

1. Do you enjoy going to see movies?
2. What is your favorite type of film?
3. When was the last time you went to the cinema? What did you see?
4. What do you think of people who talk during movies?
5. Are horror films popular in your country?
6. Are there any actors or actresses you admire?
7. On a date, would you rather see a romantic film or a comedy?
8. Do you download films from the Internet?
9. When would you prefer to watch a film at home rather than at a cinema?
10. What is the next film you want to see?

READING

1. Do you enjoy reading?
2. What do you usually like to read?
3. Do you prefer to read the news in print or online?
4. What did you like to read as child?
5. Do people in your country enjoy reading?
6. Do you often read comics? Why?
7. When was the last time you read a book?
8. What book would you recommend your friends read?

SPORTS

1. Do you enjoy playing sports? Which?
2. What sports do you like to watch on TV?
3. Which sports are popular in your country?
4. Are there any sports you don't like?
5. Is it important for a child to learn a sport?
6. Do you admire any famous athletes? Who?

TELEVISION

1. Do you like to watch TV? Why or why not?
2. What are your favorite programs?
3. Are there any shows that you don't like?
4. When do you usually watch TV?
5. Is watching TV a popular hobby for people in your country?
6. Why do people like watching TV?
7. How does watching a film on TV different from going to the cinema?
8. How do you feel about advertisements?
9. Do you use the TV to help you learn English? How?
10. What TV show from your country would you recommend to a foreigner?

FOOD AND COOKING

1. Do you enjoy cooking?
2. How often do you eat at restaurants?
3. What is your favorite food to eat?
4. What is a typical breakfast for you like?
5. Do you like food from other countries?
6. Did you eat breakfast this morning?
7. In your culture, are their special foods served during holidays?
8. What foods would you like to try but never have?
9. Is there a type of food you don't like or would never try?
10. Do you prefer to eat at home or at restaurants?
11. Are there foods you used to like, but no longer do?

TRAVELLING

1. Do you enjoy travelling? Why?

2. Where have you travelled?
3. Would you rather travel alone or with friends and family?
4. What do you dislike about travelling?
5. Describe how you prepare for a trip.
6. Do you prefer using a train or plane when you travel? Why?
7. Do people in your country enjoy travelling? Where do they usually go?
8. Where will you go on your next holiday?

MUSIC

1. Do you like music?
2. What kind of music do you like?
3. When do you usually listen to music?
4. What kind of music did you like when you were younger? What kind of music is popular in your country?
5. Do you play any musical instruments?
6. Do you wish you could play any musical instruments?
7. Which is your favorite instrument?
8. Can music change a person's mood?
9. How is music you listen to different from the music your parents listened to when they were young?
10. What makes a song "good"?
11. Do you prefer music that relaxes you or gives you energy?
12. Why do people like going to concerts?

OUTDOOR ACTIVITIES

1. What kind of outdoor activities do you enjoy?
2. Would you rather go camping in the woods or go to the beach?

3. Where do people in your country go to enjoy nature?

4. How important is it to enjoy natural beauty?

5. When was the last time you went to the beach or the mountains?

6. Describe how you prepare for a trip to the outdoors.

CITY AND COUNTRYSIDE QUESTIONS

1. Do you like living in a big city?

2. What do you like the most about city life?

3. What is your least favorite thing about living in a city?

4. What do children in your country do for fun in the countryside?

5. How does a vacation in a rural area different from one in the city?

6. What types of amenities are commonly found in small towns and villages in your country?

7. Would you prefer to live in a city or a village? Why?

8. What social problems did your hometown have when you were a child? Have these problems improved or gotten worse?

LIFESTYLE AND LEISURE QUESTIONS

1. What do you do in your free time?

2. Can you describe your typical day?

3. What do you like to do on holidays?

4. How often do visitors come to your home?

5. Do you like to read" books?

6. What is your favorite type of music?

7. Do you prefer warm or cool weather?

8. Is going to a gym popular in your country?

9. What is the best time of day for you to study?

10. Do you enjoy working in the garden?

11. When was the last time you cooked a meal?

12. Did you learn to play a musical instrument when you were younger?

13. How would you like to improve your lifestyle?

14. Do people in your country appreciate art?

PREFERENCES

1. Do you prefer watching TV or reading books?

2. Would you rather eat at home or in a restaurant?

3. How popular are comedies compared to horror films in your country?

4. Do your friends prefer to go out or stay at home on weekends?

5. Would you rather own a dog or a cat as a pet?

6. Do you prefer giving presentations or writing essays for school?

7. Would you like to visit Europe or the United States?

8. In your country, how popular are computer games compared to playing cards?

9. Would you rather get a laptop, a tablet, or a smart phone as a present?

ANIMALS

1. What is your favorite animal?

2. What was your favorite animal when you were a child?

3. Do you have a pet?
4. What animals do people keep as pets in your country?
5. Why do people keep pets?
6. Are there any animals which are symbols in your culture?
7. When was the last time you went to the zoo?
8. What are zoos like in your country?
9. Have you ever gone hunting?
10. Is hunting an important part of your country's culture?
11. Would you rather have a dog or a cat as a pet?
12. Would you like to own an exotic pet such as a snake or a tarantula?

CELL PHONES

1. How often do you use a cell phone every day?
2. Would your life be better or worse without a cell phone?
3. Do you ever send or receive text messages when you shouldn't?
4. Could you survive without a cell phone?
5. What are the worst things about cell phones?
6. What features do you look for in a cell phone?
7. Do you plan to buy a new phone?
8. How did you feel when you bought your first cell phone?

COMMUNICATION AND LANGUAGE

1. How long have you been studying English?
2. Have you studied any other languages?

3. Do you often practice another language with your friends?
4. What is the most difficult thing about learning a new language?
5. Would you rather use the Internet or a book to study a language?
6. Is your native language easy for a foreigner to learn?

EDUCATION

1. Are you currently in school? What do you study?
2. When do you usually do homework?
3. Do you enjoy studying in groups or alone? Why?
4. Is there a subject you have never studied but are interested in?
5. Who was your favorite teacher when you were a child?
6. What is your least favorite subject to study?
7. Does taking exams cause you to feel stressed?
8. How do you relieve stress when you are studying?
9. Describe your routine for doing homework.
10. Is a high-level of education valued in your country?
11. Were you involved in non-academic activities at school?
12. If you could go back to high school, what would you do differently?
13. How often do you ask a teacher for extra help?
14. What is the study environment like at your school's library?

FOOD AND COOKING

1. Do you enjoy cooking?
2. How often do you eat at restaurants?

3. What is your favorite food to eat?
4. What is a typical breakfast for you like?
5. Do you like food from other countries?
6. Did you eat breakfast this morning?
7. In your culture, are their special foods served during holidays?
8. What foods would you like to try but never have?
9. Is there a type of food you don't like or would never try?
10. Do you prefer to eat at home or at restaurants?
11. Are there foods you used to like, but no longer do?

GAMES

1. Do you enjoy playing games?
2. What sorts of games do you enjoy playing?
3. Do you prefer games where you work as a team or work alone?
4. What kinds of games did you enjoy as a child?
5. Are there any games that are traditionally popular in your country?
6. How often do you play computer games?
7. When was the last time you played a computer game?
8. What do you like about computer games? What do you dislike?

FAMILIES

1. Do you come from a large family?
2. When do you often spend time together?
3. Does your family prefer to stay home on the weekends or go out?

4. Would people in your country rather have a large or small family?

5. What special things did you do with your family as a child?

6. Do you ever practice English with a family member?

HEALTH

1. Are you a member of a health club?

2. What kinds of exercise do you do?

3. Who is the healthiest person in your family? What do they do to keep healthy?

4. Do you have a lot of stress?

5. What are some things that cause people to feel stress? What are some ways to deal with stress?

6. When was the last time you ate fast food?

7. Do you know someone who smokes? Do they plan on quitting?

8. Have you ever smoked cigarettes?

9. What disease frightens you the most? Why?

10. If you were ill, what would you do to feel healthy again?

11. What do you think of cosmetic surgery? Would you ever consider it?

FREE TIME AND HOBBIES

1. What do you like to do in your free time?

2. What hobbies did you have as a child?

3. Did your parents have any hobbies? Did you help them?

4. If you could try a new activity, what would it be?

5. Do you enjoy relaxing hobbies or exciting ones?

6. Do you have a special talent? What have you done to practice this special talent?

7. Is it better to do hobbies alone or with other people?

8. Why are hobbies important?

HOLIDAYS/ VACATIONS

1. When was the last time you went on a vacation?

2. Do you prefer- to visit familiar or new places when on a holiday?

3. Is travelling alone enjoyable for you?

4. Have you ever visited a foreign country? Where?

5. Where will you go on your next vacation?

6. If you could go anywhere, where would you go?

7. What are some popular tourist attractions in your country?

HOMETOWN

1. Where do you come from?

2. Can you tell me something about your hometown?

3. Is your hometown famous for anything?

4. What places should foreigners visit in your hometown? Why?

5. Is there anything you would like to change in your hometown?

6. What places do you like in your hometown best?

7. How has your hometown developed in the last 10 years?

8. What amenities does your town provide?

9. What are the main crops in your region?

10. What other industries are important for your hometown's economy?

1. 11 .When is the best time of year to visit your hometown?

HOUSEWORK

1. What types of household chores do you do?
2. Do you ever help with the cooking?
3. Is there a certain time that you do housework?
4. Are you good at any particular household task?
5. What is your least favorite chore to do?
6. If you could avoid doing a specific chore, what would it be?

THE INTERNET

1. How often do you use the Internet?
2. What was your first experience with the Internet like?
3. What do you mainly use it for?
4. Tell me about your favorite website.
5. Do you use Facebook or twitter?
6. What is your least favorite thing about the Internet?
7. Would you rather watch films online or at the cinema?
8. Do you like to access the Internet on your mobile phone?
9. What do you think about "blogging"?
10. Have you ever uploaded a video to Youtube.com?

MONEY

1. Are you good at saving money?

2. What do you usually spend your money on?

3. How often do you go shopping?

4. Do you ever use a credit card?

5. Would you rather shop at a mall or a small market?

6. What do you 4hink about online shopping?

7. When was the last time you shopped for clothing?

8. Is fashion important to you?

9. What is the most expensive thing you have ever bought?

10. How is shopping alone different from shopping with friends?

11. Tell me about your favorite shop.

12. Are there some shops that you refuse to spend money at? Why?

DESCRIBING HABITS

1. What do you like to cook?

2. What did you like to watch on TV when you were a child?

3. Where do you spend time with your friends?

4. What kind of clothes do you like to wear?

5. Do you ever do charity work?

6. How often do you read the newspaper?

7. When do you usually do housework?

8. What sports did you play when you were growing up?

9. Who do you practice English with?

10. Do you enjoy singing karaoke?

11. Which foods don't you like?
12. Did you help your mother with household tasks when you were a teenager?

COMPUTERS

1. How often do you use a computer?
2. What are your favorite things to do on a computer?
3. Do you enjoy playing computer games?
4. Did you have difficulties the first time you used a computer?
5. Does the computer ever distract you from completing important tasks?
6. What is your opinion regarding social networking sites?
7. Can you tell me about your favorite website?
8. Do you use a computer to study English? How?

FUTURE PLANS

1. Why are you taking the IELTS test?
2. What are you planning to do in the next five years?
3. What are you planning to do in the next ten years?
4. What is the first thing you will do when you arrive at the new place?

THE SEA

1. Have you ever made a journey by boat?
2. Is the seaside a popular destination for people in your country?

3. What do you think should be done to prevent pollution of the oceans?

4. Do you enjoy going to the beach?

5. When you go to the beach, what do you normally do?

MODERN LIFE

1. Is life in your country today very different from when your grandparents were your age?

2. What things are changing in your country at the moment? Do you think modern life is healthy?

3. Where do people from your country like to go on vacation?

4. Have you ever been abroad? Did you enjoy it?

WEATHER AND SEASONS

1. What seasons do you have in your country?

2. Which season do most people go away on holiday in your country? Why?

3. Which season do you like the most? Why?

PART 2 SPEAKING INTRODUCTION

When part 1 speaking is finished; this means after the examiner has asked you a series of questions on three different topics *(work, study, where are you living, and the two other topics)*, they are going to move to part 2 speaking, they will give you a direction, they will explain exactly what they are doing, everything is very clear in part 2 speaking. The examiner will be giving you a card, and the card will have a task on it. They want you to talk about something.

What do they want you to talk about?

That will be **NOUNS**: people, places, things like objects that you own, objects that you would like to own, events (things that you did in the past, for example, *graduation ceremony, grandpa's birthday, etc.*)

The examiner will give you a card and ask you to describe something, someone, a place, or an event, and your job is to take this card and you are going to talk about the card for 2 minutes. Another word is that you are going to give a short speech. They are **not** asking you questions in part 2 speaking. It's different from part 1 speaking (questions and answers). In part 2 speaking, just has answer, no question.

When the examiner gives you a card, they also give you a piece of paper and a pencil or a pen to take notes. You will have 1 minute to look at the card and think about what you are going to say and you can take notes in that 1 minute. Remember that you can use the notes to read and look at while you are speaking. You must talk about the topic on the card, but you can freely talk about anything. They will make this card general enough that everyone can talk about. So they are **not** going to say *"talk about your favorite city in Egypt"*, so it's never so specific. Instead, they just ask you to *"talk about your favorite city"*. Everyone can think about their favorite city. It's very general. It's a good idea to talk about the topic points in order. Here is the thing, before you are talking about something is challenging on the card because part 2 will offer some unique challenging points, I want you to start thinking about simple points on the card first. These are basic questions because you can add a question mark to these, change the words around and these are all questions. These are actually part 1 speaking questions.

Example:

Do you have a favorite book?

Yes, I really love Harry Porter

Who wrote it?

This book was written by J. K. Rowling. She is a British author who is now very famous for writing this book.

What happens in the book?

Well, a lot of things are happening in the book. Basically, it's about a boy, Harry, who discovers he has a magical power...

When did you read it?

I first read this book since I was 14 years old...

What I am doing here is I am trying to produce extended answers to part 1 speaking questions. That's a key here. **Do not** think of this as a 2-minute speech; that's too much. Instead, think of it as 10 seconds, 10 seconds, 20 seconds, 20 seconds, 20 seconds, and 20 seconds. Little pieces are more important.

There are some challenges in part 2 speaking. One of the big challenges coming up with an idea is that you don't know what they are going to give you on a card. It could be anything. Some things are easy to prepare for, other things are weird.

For example: *Are you ready to talk about your favorite comic actor?* **May be not.**

Who is the comic actor? You might **not be ready** to talk about this topic, and in order to choose a good thing to talk about is also a challenge.

The other thing is taking notes and using them. The only purpose of these notes is for you. You don't receive a band score for taking notes. The examiner will not collect it, and they will throw it into the trash. So the only purpose that the notes have is for you to be using while you are speaking. You don't have to write sentences on your piece of paper because you have very limited time. Instead, you should write keywords, and 1, 2 or 3 phrases that when you look at the words, they give you ideas for other things to talk about.

So if you are going to answer *"why is it your favorite book?"*

You could say: ***it's exciting***, and then explain why it is exciting by looking at your notes and start talking. Looking at keywords will allow you to talk a lot of things about your favorite book.

Sample answer:

Today I'm gonna tell you about Harry porter, one of my favorite books. This novel is written by J. K. Rowling. She is now a famous British author. In fact, this was the first book that she ever wrote. In this book, I meet my hero Harry Porter, he is a young boy who finds out that he has a magical power, therefore he goes to school to develop his power and learn skills that using poison…..I first read this book 15 years ago during the winter time when the weather was really cold outside. I got this book for Christmas, my friend had recommended it to me because he had read it and really enjoyed it…I love this book because it's so exciting. What I mean is there are a lot of amazing adventures and powers…it's really well written, and has a lot of interesting things to read. And finally, I really like Harry, he is a really friendly and charming boy…..actually, I really like to read this book.

Answer structure: *Explaining -- adding ideas -- explaining -- examples*

Another challenge in part 2 speaking is a lack of question. In part 2 speaking, there is no question, so what you need to do is to show the examiner *where you are talking about? How you are talking? Signal and pause* can allow you to be a lot more organized, take a breath and allow the examiner to easily find you while you are speaking.

How the examiner marks you in part 2 speaking:

- **Coherence and cohesion:** are you *speaking smoothly* (not ~~too quickly~~) and *in an organized way* that is *easy to understand.*
- **Vocabulary:** are you using *a wide range of words, verb forms?* Are you *being descriptive?* Are you *paraphrasing?* Is your *vocabulary accurate?*

- **Grammar:** sentence structures; *concession & contrast*; *conditionals* (it depends…); *verb tenses* (using a range of verb tenses); *verb forms*; *adjectives* (be descriptive + explain adjectives); *referencing & pronouns*.
- **Pronunciation** (focus on the *final sounds, intonation, word stress*)

PART 2 SPEAKING TIPS

Remember to include a clear introduction and conclusion to your Part 2 speech.

Introduction:

- *I'm going to describe...*
- *The X I would like to describe...*
- *I'm going to talk about an X (in my country called the...)*

Conclusion:

- *That's why the ... is such a famous building.*
- *It's a very famous X not only within my country but also abroad.*
- *It's such a special X because...*

Continuation:

If you find yourself having nothing to say in the middle of your talk, take a moment to refocus by using one of the useful phrases like:

- *Let me think...*
- *Well,...*
- *Actually,...*
- *I can't quite remember the ...*
- *I think ...*
- *I mean...*
- *Basically,...*
- *Anyway, ...*

Do you need eye contact in IELTS speaking?

There is nothing in the IELTS exam that has anything about eye contact. Of course, you want to keep some eye contact with the examiner. This is polite but you've got some notes in front of you that you took, you've got the card in front of you. You're speaking, you're reading the notes, and you're thinking about more things to say. You've got a lot of things going on. In the exam, this is quite more important. Looking at the examiner and keeping some eye contact with him **is NOT important**. I would say if you worry about it, you should *stay focused, stay focused, stay focused* and *look at the examiner every once in a while*. When the examiner gives you a minute to take notes, take your notes. The examiner will tell you when your time is up. Please don't take notes and say *"can I have more time?"* – It **never happens**. Likewise, when your 1 minute is up, the examiner will say *"your time is up"*, and now you can start your speaking.

The keyword of part 2 speaking is *being organized, being organized and being organized* so the examiner can follow what you are talking about and *try to be influent, try to produce a lot of English for 2 minutes*. Be strict with your time when you practice, don't ever give your short speech for over 2 minutes.

Most common things we usually do in part 2 speaking is **a place, a person, an event, an experience, or an object.**

If you are describing **a place**, you should provide some details like *where is it located? When did you first go there? What does it look like? What happened there? Why you were there? What you did there? How did you feel about this place? Why did you remember this place so well? What do you remember the most about this place? Why do you think this place is so beautiful?*

Pay attention to the verb tenses (present tense, past tense…)

PEOPLE DESCRIPTION

When you describe a person, you should try to use <u>adjectives of evaluation</u> and <u>adjectives of personality</u>.

- *Who the person is?* (Relatives or friend...)
  I would like to talk about <u>my grandmother</u>.
  I would like to talk about <u>my favorite history teacher</u>.
  I would like to talk about <u>my next door neighbor</u>.
- *What do they do?* (occupation)
- *Social position* (what do they do in society?)
- *How do you know them?*
- *What they are like* (using <u>adjectives of personality</u> & <u>explain the adjectives</u>).
  If you tell the examiner someone is <u>strict and hardworking</u>, <u>give them examples about how they are strict and hardworking</u> *"I admire my father, but sometimes he is quite strict. What I mean is if I am 5 minutes late for dinner, he makes me give him a dollar"*. So what you should do is you need to have an explanation because if you don't, it makes the listener naturally feel like that <u>they are missing something</u>. Imagine that you have a conversation with your friend. He is very polite, and he asks you *"how was your holiday?"* and you say *"well, I had a lot of fun. I went to London. It's very interesting"*. Then, certainly, your friend will be asking to himself *"interesting? How?"* what do you mean for "interesting"? So, you must explain your adjectives. You <u>don't need to use a lot of adjectives</u>, you <u>just need maybe 2, maybe 3 adjectives but you must explain them</u>.
  If you just throw out the adjectives *"Oh, I love my father because he is so humorous, friendly, hardworking, thrifty..."* that means you are just <u>listing</u> and certainly that's <u>not impressive</u>; that <u>doesn't sound natural</u>.
- *What they have achieved* (using <u>phrases of achievement</u>). These are used a lot in part 2 speaking because in part 2 speaking, we usually talk about people that we like or we admire and we have relationship with)

PHRASES THAT TALK ABOUT WORKING HARD:

Through sheer hard work, he has built up his company

My mother was not very successful in high school, but she *persevered* and graduated from university. Now she is a doctor.

PHRASES THAT TALK ABOUT SUCCESS:

He *has the will to succeed*.

Something I admire about Barack Obama is he *earned a respect of people* who met him.

PHRASES THAT TALK ABOUT TALENT:

He *has a gift for* playing guitar.

He *has a gift for* kicking football.

My mother *has a gift for* cooking.

PHRASES THAT TALK ABOUT ADMIRATION:

I really *appreciate* what my father did for me.

I will always *look up to/ admire/ respect* him for his work.

I *think highly of/ proud of* my father and his work.

EXPRESSIONS HOPING TO IMITATE SOMEBODY:

I hope I am as + adjective + as + person

I hope I will be as + adjective + as + person

I hope I am *as successful as* my father is when I grow up

I hope I am *as beautiful as* my mother is when I grow up.

I hope I will be *as wealthy as* Bill Gates.

EXPRESSIONS OF IMITATION:

<u>I would like to be as intelligent as</u> my grandfather.

<u>I would like to be as beautiful as</u> my grandfather.

<u>I would like to be as wealthy as</u> Bill Gates.

ADJECTIVES OF PERSONALITY

NEGATIVE PERSONALITY ADJECTIVES LIST

Aggressive: He has a real passive *aggressive* personality/ he had a very *aggressive* attitude.

Arrogant: He was so *arrogant* that he thought he could tell everyone what to do.

That girl is *arrogant* because of her beauty.

Bitchy: She can be really *bitchy* sometimes.

Boastful: Peter was too *boastful* when describing his new bike.

Boring: I don't like Tom because he is *boring* and unfriendly.

Bossy: I dislike her because she is *bossy*.

Careless: Although he is brave, he is *careless*.

Changeable: She is *changeable* and stubborn.

Conservative: He is not as *conservative* as he used to be.

Cowardly: Tom is shy and *cowardly*.

Nervous: He was *nervous* so he forgot her name.

Obsessive: He was *obsessive* about food and coffee.

Overemotional: She was *overemotional* in public.

Pessimistic: He is *pessimistic* about the future

Quick-tempered: My brother is *quick-tempered* and impatient.

Resentful: She is *resentful* about being demoted.

Others: Rude, selfish, silly, stingy, sneaky, stubborn, timid, unkind, unreliable, unkind, immature, short-temper = irritable, frugal = thrifty, cruel, deceitful, dishonest, evil, flirtatious, foolish, fussy, greedy, grumpy, impatient, impolite, inconsiderate, intolerant, inflexible, indecisive, lazy, jealous, materialistic, mean, moody, narrow-minded, naughty, nasty, etc.

POSITIVE PERSONALITY ADJECTIVES LIST

Affectionate: *She is affectionate to her animals.*

Ambitious: *He is ambitious to succeed.*

Friendly: *Tom is friendly to everyone.*

Amiable: *He is amiable and gracious.*

Funny: *Joe is funny.*

Generous: *My father is generous with his money.*

Gentle: *She is gentle with children.*

Brave: *Peter is brave, and Tom is humorous.*

Bright: *My nephew is bright.*

Broad-minded: *He is broad-minded and straightforward.*

Hard-working: *She is a very intelligent and hardworking student.*

Charming: *She is charming and beautiful.*

Humorous: *I think Tom is humorous.*

Sociable: *He is a sociable, reliable man.*

Others: communicative, compassionate, impartial, passionate, patient, persistent, polite, powerful, practical, pro-active, reliable, romantic, self-confident, self-disciplined, sincere, sociable, straightforward, sympathetic, thoughtful, tidy, tough, understanding, versatile, warmhearted, willing, witty , adaptable, fair-minded, passionate, adventurous, faithful, persistent, independent, romantic, considerate, intellectual, smart = intelligent, supportive, charitable, approachable.

PEOPLE DESCRIPTION MODEL ANSWER

SAMPLE 1:

Describe a person (you know), much older than you, who you admire.

You should say:

Who this person is

How you know this person

How this person has influenced you

And explain why you admire this person.

MODEL ANSWER:

Today I'm gonna talk about one of my favorite teachers who taught me at high school. Her name is Taylor. She had a great influence on me and was the most well-mannered person whom I look up to very much. Ms. Taylor taught me English for 3 years of high school. She was in her 40s, and she had a lot of teaching experience. In fact, we met each other almost every day since she was also my form teacher. She was always kind to students, treated us with respect and cared about us as if we had been her children. To be specific, she always brought some kinds of medicines so that whenever any student had a cold, cough or something like that, she would give them the medicines immediately.

Above all, the way she taught us in class influenced me the most. Her thoroughness and dedication in teaching inspired me to study English, even though I had not been interested in this foreign language before. Thanks to her inspiring teaching method, I was able to pass the university entrance exam with a high English grade. Moreover, she was very friendly and approachable, far more than I expected, in fact. She was willing to share her ideas and answer to all my questions. I was also influenced by her lifestyle, which was so worthy of respect and simple that I really wanted to imitate her. As she is a kind person, she always gave us the best advice and solutions about any problems we faced. From time to time, I felt that she was like my close friend who I could comfortably share everything with.

Although we have now all graduated from high school and have different goals to chase in life, we usually visit her at the weekends to share with her about our daily life at college.

SAMPLE 2:

Describe your good friend.

You should say:

Who this person is

Who long you have known them (= him or her)

Or, how you first met what you do together

And explain why you think this person is a good friend

MODEL ANSWER:

Speaking of a good friend, I would like to talk about Lucy, whom I have known for roughly 5 years. I first met her at university when she was my classmate. She was smart, confident, thoughtful, and always a straight A student who used to be nominated as the president of the student union because of her excellent academic performance. Moreover, she can always give me a helping hand and the most sincere advice whenever I am in need. For example, I remember when I didn't pass the mock university entrance exam, she consoled me, found the best ways to inspire me and made me more motivated in study and then we studied together until the official exam took place. Finally, with our effort we passed the entrance examination and studied at our favorite college.

At present, despite the fact that we have different plans and goals to pursue, I strongly believe that we will try our best to maintain this relationship and we will be best friends for good. Indeed, Lucy is a real friend of mine.

MODEL SENTENCES FOR PEOPLE DESCRIPTION

…I admire him/her from the bottom of my heart not only because of the person himself/herself, but also because of the things I learned from his/her words…

…I love/ impress/ admire my grandpa not only because of the person himself, but also because of the interesting, friendly, kind personality he has…

… His/her words influenced me a lot/very much…

…He/she never gives up easily…

…I hope that I will be able to become an inspirational person like him one day…

… He/she is a well-known investor/businessman…

… He/she has also made a great contribution to charity…

… He/she looks much younger than he/she actually is…

… He/she is of medium build and medium height….

…My father/grandpa/uncle is a very modern and interesting person….

…He/she is really into taking pictures, collecting antiques, and travelling around the world…

…He/she left me a lot of beautiful childhood memories…

…He/she took really good care of me when I was little; cooked me my favourite food, played with me, walked me to school and home, told me fairy tales, …

….My grandma/grandpa is a really nice person….

…. We have a lot in common and are like peas and carrots (get along very well together)…..

….He/she has been a real friend to me….

… He/she always gives me a listening ear, a helping hand and the most sincere words/advice whenever I am in need…..I felt much better after talking to her/him….

…. The saying that a near neighbour is better than a distant cousin is totally true….

….. She is very beautiful. She has curly blonde hair, big blue eyes and a straight high nose. I bet you couldn't take your eyes off her if you saw her in person….

….He/she is easy-going, knowledgeable, thoughtful and inspirational…..

… He/she is a person with a strong sense of humour…

…He/she has a good sense of orientation/ direction….

…Apart from being excellent in…, he/she is also good at…

…He/ she is very persistent until he/she succeeds….

…He/she is one of the most important and influential people in my life…..

…I feel that he/she is a knowledgeable person….

…He/she is able to explain something complicated in an easy and simple way….

…He/she is always nice and gentle to people around him…

….She dresses up nicely, does a gorgeous hairstyle, wears beautiful makeup and high heels.

…I really admire and appreciate her/his diligence and responsibility…

…He/she is also known as a charitable person…

…He/she is really a role model for me to learn from…

…He/she is able to get along well with all types of people…

…My mother has an eye for fashion. She usually keeps up with the latest fashion…

…He/she became successful after many years of writing songs/books…

…He/she tried to keep me entertained and find interesting things for us to do together…

…He/she has always taught me to be more patient and understanding towards other people…

PLACE DESCRIPTION

ANSWER ORDER:

1. What it is *(a shopping mall that/which is)*
2. Where it is *(near, close to, next to, across from, behind, on the corner of, at the end of the street, on X Street)*.
3. When you first go there *(I first went there 10 years ago)*
4. What it looks like *(a crowded place -- being descriptive)*
5. What is it famous for *(this place is famous for/ this place is renowned for seafood, noodle, clean streets)*
6. Why do you visit this place *(because it provided me with something (delicious food, information, advice, etc./ I love going to the zoo because this gives me a chance to relax and see animals ("this" refers to "going to the zoo")/ ...because it reminds me of.../ because it lets me escape from daily life routines..../ .... because it makes me feel...)*
7. How do you feel about this place. *(My uncle's house is very important to me because I spend a lot of time there on the weekend/ I found this place very beautiful because it's so relaxing/ The sounds that you hear coming from the ocean are very soothing/ In fact, when I was there I watched two birds singing to each other....).*

ADJECTIVES FOR DESCRIBING PLACES

- **Enchanting:** *El Nido has been the most enchanting place I have ever visited.*

- **Attractive and enjoyable:** *We want to make the town a more attractive and enjoyable place for visitors.*

- **Stimulating:** *The swimming is stimulating.*

- **Cozy** = inviting # uncomfortable: *This coffee shop is cozy.*

- **Quiet** = peaceful # bustling: *Sometimes I need a quiet place to escape from my daily life routines.*

- **Vibrant** = lively # boring: *Art gallery is a lively place.*

- **Hectic:** *The restaurant is hectic.*

- **Boring** = dull # fascinating

- **Traditional** = old-fashioned # modern

- **Exhilarating**

- **Charming**

- **Impressive**

QUESTION ANALYSE:

Describe a place that your parent took you to

What sort of place it was *(a recreational area, a shopping mall, a restaurant, a cinema, a park, a religious building, a temple, etc.)*

How you got there *(my family and I took a bus…)*

Why your parents took you there (what is the reason: *vacation, to visit my uncle; attend my cousin's wedding…)*

Why you would or would not take your own children to this place *(if I had children, I'd take them here because I had a lot of fun/ because it's very beautiful/*

because I think they would have as much fun as I did.)

PLACE DESCRIPTION MODEL ANSWER

SAMPLE 1:

Describe a place with a lot of water (such as a river, a lake or the ocean) that you enjoyed visiting.

You should say:

Where this place was

What you did there

Why you went there

Who you went there with

And explain why you liked this place.

ANSWER:

I would like to talk about a place where my family went on a vacation last summer. It's called Binh Ba Island, which is located in Nha Trang city and I was really impressed with the beach there. The scenery along the coast was just breathtaking.

When we arrived at this destination, we had to take a ferry from the mainland, a journey which lasted roughly one hour. Fortunately, I was not seasick. When we reached there, surprisingly, the scenery appealed to me a lot, particularly the beach. The beach itself was absolutely breathtaking and the crystal clear water seemed to stretch endlessly to the horizon. Moreover, from a distance, huge waves were crashing onto the shore, which sounded like a melody. I was so excited that I just wanted to jump into the sea immediately.

On the beach, many people were enjoying the scenery, and some were swimming while their children were making sandcastles. My family quickly checked into the hotel, we changed our clothes and joined the people there.

Actually, this vacation provided me a great chance to relax myself and escape from my daily life routines after a long hard time at work. Personally, I hope that I will have more holidays like this in the future.

SAMPLE 2:

Describe a quiet place.

Where it is

How often you visit there

What you do there

And explain the reason why you like or dislike the place.

ANSWER:

To me, quiet places mean libraries. But I'm not going to describe the library at my university as I still haven't visited it yet. The one I'm going to describe is the library at my high school in Sydney.

My school is very large and it consists of four big blocks named A, B, C, and D. The library occupies a small space on the highest floor in block D, and it's perhaps just about three or nearly four times as large as a normal classroom. There's a room used to store books and another for students to read books and self-study.

I spent most of my time in the library when I was in grade 10. The next two years were filled completely with competitions and extracurricular activities so I couldn't go to the library as often as before. I had my own favorite spot in the self-study section; it was the cubicle on the outermost row that is near the window, and whenever I visited the library to study or to read some borrowed books, I would choose that spot without any hesitation. I even wrote some words or symbols that I liked on the table; don't know whether they're still there now though.

I specifically chose this library to describe because it's really quiet, compared with some other libraries in Sydney that I've been to. It was really suitable for studying, and some students even went there to sleep! I had a great time self-studying in this library back then, I seriously would visit it again if I ever had a chance.

MODEL SENTENCES FOR PLACE DESCRIPTION

....Decoration style is classy and upscale....

....Atmosphere is cozy and comfy....

....Food is tasty and flavourful....

....The service is hospitable and speedy. All orders can be served in 10 minutes....

....The hotel was designed and constructed by the architects from South Africa, and took approximately ten years to complete....

....Food prices are affordable....

....Its location is convenient. It is easy to find a parking space....

....A customer can feel very comfy in such an environment....

....The restaurant is spacious. We can have different options when choosing a seat, and it also leaves some privacy for talking; it is pretty customer-oriented....

....The most impressive part about this spectacular building is its distinctive shape, which gives everyone an impression that a boat is sailing on the sea....

....What impressed me most was the hotel we stayed at....

....The hotel is definitely a unique symbol for Dubai....

....When I actually saw the hotel, I was totally amazed by it....

....The hotel gave us an impression that a boat was sailing on the sea....

....It makes the hotel iconic and unique....

….The library is situated in the center of the campus….

….The coffee house is located on a quiet street with a lot of trees planted on both sides….

….It is on the opposite side of my university….

….You can see a huge collection of books of different kinds: journals, academic books, magazines, newspapers….

….There is a cozy cafe on the top floor. It is great to sit down, enjoy the lovely campus view, and taste my favourite cappuccino while reading the book….

….When I was little, the room I loved the most was my bedroom….

….All the walls were painted light yellow, which made the room look elegant and subtle….

….My parents even hung a lot of photos of my family on the walls….

….This park is also a popular place for walking, jogging, flying a kite, playing hide-and-seek, having a picnic, dog walking, fishing…

….The scene is so spectacular when all the cherry blossoms are in full blossom in spring….

….The water is wonderfully clear….

….The most amazing scene is the time when cherry blossom petals fall down all over the river like snowflakes….

….It is the greatest place for relaxation….

….I love this park not only because of the park itself, but also because of the atmosphere I can soak up in the park….

….The room was equipped with central air-conditioning, satellite TV and internet access, which was very convenient….

….This place is quite private….

…. This is a lively, fashionable and cosmopolitan place…..

….A lot of public events and private parties are held in this place as well….

….The restaurant I would like to talk about is called Pizza Hut, which is a western-style restaurant, specializing in pizza and spaghetti. It is one of the most popular and famous restaurants in Japanese nowadays….

….Well, the foreign country that I would like to visit is the UK, which is one of the most attractive and fascinating travelling destinations for many backpackers, and I am no exception….

….It is also an ideal place for me to meet and chat with my relatives….

OBJECT DESCRIPTION

Something that comes up in part 2 speaking is talking about objects, talking about things that you own like *a watch, a smartphone, a motorbike, etc*. When we talk about an object, we need to describe its appearance.

How do we describe its appearance? We describe it by using adjectives. But you know, there are a lot of things you can say about objects. We can talk about what we think about it. *Is it beautiful? Is it lovely? Is it ugly?*...We can talk about *its size*, we can be general, we can say *big, small, tiny*...we can be specific (3 centimeter long, 2 feet long...). We can talk about *its age* like new, old, brand-new, twelve years old; we can talk about *its shape, color*; we can also talk about *its pattern*; we can talk about *its origin (where is it from?)*; we can talk about *its material (wood, bamboo, metal..)*

Made of & made from: these prepositions are very important.

We use **made of** when we can still recognize the material that is used to make the object.

For example: *the house is made of wood*.

We use **made from** when we don't know what material is used to make the object.

For example: *Plastic is made from oil*.

When we are talking about the description about where we got something, or how we found something, we are going to talk about the past, but we don't just stick with past simple, and past simple. We should be saying something like *"I was visiting my family when my brother surprised me with a new watch"* or sorts of reasons (ways to talk about **why** or **what** was your object is used by using *infinitive of purpose "to; in order to; so as to"*), and then we can talk about when was the first time, when was the last time we saw or used something. For example *"the first time I used this computer when I was 10 years old"*, *"the last time I saw the watch is when I was at my parents' home"*; *"the last time I played the video game was with my brother at Christmas 4 years ago"*, and then we will talk about how this object made us or other people feel? You might talk about the birthday present you received or you might talk about the birthday present you gave. Either way, there will be interested how you feel about giving it or how the other feels about getting it. In this case, you should talk about <u>what the object looks like</u>, but you also talk about what other people feel, and why other people do things by <u>using adjectives of evaluation</u> *"people watch TV because it's relaxing"*, *"people like to read because it's enjoyable"* we use adjectives of evaluation to talk about <u>what we feel</u>, and <u>how we feel</u>.

USEFUL ADJECTIVES FOR DESCRIBING OBJECTS

Opinion: good, wonderful, splendid, pretty, fantastic, awful, ugly, dirty, comfortable, uncomfortable, wasteful, valuable, worthless, worthy, useful, useless, important, scarce, rare, lovely, disgusting, amazing, loathsome, surprising, usual, unusual, etc.

Touch: hard, silky, soft, smooth, polished, grainy, rough, glossy, glassy, etc.

Size, weight: heavy, small, tiny, little, light, big, tall, fat, short, slender, thin, underweight, wide, enormous, vast, giant, huge, great, slim, etc.

Smell: perfumed, smelly, noxious, aromatic, fragrant, scented, etc.

Temperature: hot, cold, icy, freezing, frigid, etc.

Age: old, young, baby, teenage, adolescent, antique, ancient, youthful, old-fashioned, elderly, mature, modern, recent, etc.

Shape: round, circular, triangular, square, oval, spherical, sleek, straight, wavy, etc.

Brightness: light, bright, dark, shining, dull, pale, glowing, gleaming, luminous, etc.

Color: blue, black, purple, white, red, pink, orange, dark green, yellowish, gray, silver, brown, transparent, colorless, etc.

Material: cloth, fabric, concrete, ceramic, metal, china, cotton, glass, plastic, wooden, steel, leather, silicon,...

OBJECT DESCRIPTION MODEL ANSWER

Describe a product you bought that you were (or, are) happy with.

You should say:

What you bought

How you bought it

Why you bought it

And explain why you were (or are) happy with it.

MODEL ANSWER 1:

I would like to talk about a household appliance which <u>plays an integral part</u> of my daily life, and <u>makes me very satisfied with</u>; that is a washing machine.

<u>Thanks to the simple instructions</u>, and this machine is <u>very easy to use</u>, my family members and I use it every day to wash our laundries such as clothing or sheets.

Personally, I think this machine <u>is quite beneficial to me due to its convenience</u>. <u>To be specific</u>, instead of spending nearly an hour on cleaning clothing by hand, it takes me only 5 minutes to put all the clothing in a washing machine. <u>Moreover</u>, my clothes washer has a large capacity up to 15kg so I can run a load of clothing through it at one time <u>in order to</u> save both water and time. <u>As a result</u>, I can save a huge amount of time <u>in order to</u> do other household chores or even learn new things that <u>I'm interested in</u>; <u>for example</u>, I can learn foreign languages or cooking.

<u>In addition</u>, a washing machine can dry clothing automatically; <u>therefore</u>, I don't have to worry about my clothing will be wet in the rainy season or winter.

<u>As a final point, I would say that</u> the washing machine is one of the greatest inventions of the industrial revolution that brings various benefits for me and other people using it.

MODEL ANSWER 2:

I would like to talk about a Samsung smart phone which I bought last summer and I was really satisfied with it. This cell phone was the latest product from Samsung, so there were various useful applications such as video calling, camera, Zalo chat, emails, games, music players, and so on. I would use this smart phone to listen to music, make phone calls, send messages and check emails. I must say that this portable device helps me a lot no matter where I am.

There were various reasons why I loved this product. Firstly, I would use it for entertainment purposes. What I mean is I could refresh myself after a long hard day at work by listening to my favorite music or enjoying action movies online. Moreover, thanks to this smart phone, I was able to keep in touch with my old friends whom I didn't often have a chance to meet in person. In addition, this mobile phone helped me to handle my workload effectively. For example, I could check and send emails or write my essays when waiting for the bus, which saved a huge amount of my time.

At present, I still use this smart phone every day for my work, study, and entertainment purposes. I think that this is an indispensable product in my daily life routines.

MODEL SENTENCES FOR OBJECT DESCRIPTION

....I love it because it can **release my stress, relieve my pressure and** put me in a good mood....

....**It was** super thin and incredibly light....

....**I was totally impressed by**....

....**It is a photo of my whole family** sitting around the table having New Year's Dinner....

....**The photo always reminds me of** the meal my mom cooked and the words my father said before the dinner....

....**I love it not only because of** the toy itself, **but also the sentimental value it has to me**....

....**Its color is** super eye-catching....

....**It was** an original oil painting **on canvas**....

....**I remember that** the first time I read the book **was around October 2010**....

....**I am interested in this vehicle for a number of reasons**....

....**This vehicle is** quite fashionable and trendy....

....**The quality is** reliable and trustworthy....

....**Its price is** affordable....

....**The one I choose is my baby girl doll,** which was one of my favorite toys as a child....

....**I didn't actually buy this smartphone because it** would be too expensive for me to afford. It was a gift from my uncle....

....The church is made of red brick, and the architecture, as I said before, is in the old French style....

....A folding chair is convenient for me because my room is small and I don't have space for a lot of furniture....

....When I first saw the bicycle I was very excited....

....It was a birthday present from my parents....

....It has various applications like video chat, digital camera, wireless Internet, and games. It's easy to share photos and music....

....I use this smartphone for almost everything, it even has a calendar that reminds me about appointments....

....This smartphone is an essential part of my life. I couldn't live without it....

....This Lego car was a birthday present from my parents....

....Last summer I bought a new smartphone and I am very satisfied with it....

....The most important thing is that this smartphone is very easy to use....

....There were numerous reasons why I took an interest in this smartphone. Firstly, I would like to use it for entertainment purposes....

....This household appliance plays an important role in my daily life....

....The coat is made of cotton only and by a Japanese clothes brand....

PAST EVENT DESCRIPTION

ANSWER ORDER:

1. What it was *(a historic event, a party, a ceremony, a wedding, a bicycle tour, a family holiday, a vacation, a kind of weather, a TV program, a football match, summer camp, school trip etc.)*
2. When it happened *(last week, last month, last year, in December, since I was a teenager, 2 years ago, on my parents' 20th wedding anniversary, at Christmas, etc.)*
3. Where it happened *(in the countryside, on the street, at the university, at my uncle's house, at a restaurant, etc.)*
4. What happened *(dancing, singing, drinking, playing games, telling jokes, cooking, etc.)*
5. Who was there *(my family, friends, teachers, neighbors, classmates, farmers, my cousin, etc.)*
6. How you feel/felt about it *(relaxing, enjoyable, valuable, special, embarrassed, moved, delighted, thrilled, enthusiastic, satisfied etc.)*

PAST EVENT DESCRIPTION MODEL ANSWER

SAMPLE 1:

Describe a sporting event that you have attended.

You should say:

What kind of sporting event it was

When the event took place

What you did there & who was with you

And explain how you felt about it.

MODEL ANSWER:

I'm gonna talk about an absurd boxing match that I along with my best friend went to watch last week. To be honest, since I realized that I was quite physically unfit, and I thought that I should take up regular exercise, so I have taken up boxing to get into shape. This has led me to develop my fondness for this kind of sport, and I decided to go and watch a real bout.

As it was the final of the local competition, the two contestants were both extremely competent. While we were waiting for the boxers to come into the ring, crowds of spectators started to cheer and chant enthusiastically to show their support for the two fighters, which created an exciting atmosphere of participation. 15 minutes later, the boxers appeared. They looked incredibly muscular, and this made me green with envy of their athletic physique.

Since boxing involves a high possibility of injury, on safety grounds both athletes were sufficiently equipped with essential sports gear for their protection, which may be one reason why the sport continues to thrive, despite the dangers. After the introduction and rules reminder, the contest started. It was interesting that the two participants were equally talented, so they had to really exert themselves to win. However, just at the height of the contest, one boxer got a cramp and tripped unexpectedly. The fall was so sudden that he couldn't react and ended up spraining his wrist. Although it was not a life-threatening injury, it did prevent him from continuing the fight. The other fighter was then declared the winner. Everybody was at a loss for words, and I have to say that was the most interesting match I've ever seen! It was a little disappointing, but also funny and fascinating in a way.

Personally, this match was quite entertaining and valuable for me. I learnt a lot of remarkable skills from the boxers; they were so professional. I hope I will be as skillful as they are, and I will definitely practice my skills regularly from now.

SAMPLE 2:

Describe a time you had good experience in the countryside

You should say

Where it was

When it was

What you did

And explain why you liked/disliked the experience

MODEL ANSWER:

Although I live in a very hectic city, I also feel connected to the countryside. Life in the rural areas always brings me a sense of tranquility. Last summer, I got away from the overcrowded city by spending all the time with my grandparents in the country. This experience has been a great memory for me to look back on with fondness.

Well, as you can imagine, country life is quite different from that of the city, and living in the countryside is sometimes really challenging. While in my city apartment, all I have to do is just some light housework like washing dishes or cleaning the bathroom, but in the countryside, I have to take care of the garden every day and even help out with farm work. My grandparents have instructed me to do this because it will help to develop self-reliance. Although there are some hardships involved, finishing these tasks brings me closer to nature and I have gradually become more adaptable to changes. Besides, without the distraction of the Internet, I found myself more open to people around me and understand them better. I have come to realize that alienation between humans nowadays is partly caused by the dominance of technology.

Despite getting back to my normal life in the city, I still find the time spent in the countryside very memorable. I believe that thanks to the precious time spent in my grandparents' country home, I have become more mature and dependable.

SAMPLE 3:

Describe a time you talked to a stranger

You should say:

Who the person was

Where the conversation took place

What the conversation was about

And explain why you found the conversation exciting.

MODEL ANSWER:

Last month, on the flight to Tokyo, I had a chance to talk to a British environmentalist, and I have to say that it was a very memorable conversation. During the conversation, she enlightened me as to the seriousness of our environmental problems. Practically, she said that the relentless exploitation of human beings has depleted a lot of natural resources, such as forests, water, plants and, of course, fossil fuels. Moreover, problems like global warming also stem from various kinds of pollution, the most severe of which is air pollution. Undoubtedly, these environmental problems would be extremely detrimental to our health, and affect overall standards of living and quality of life.

When I asked her about how to alleviate such environmental problems, she said the decisive factor is our awareness. People should bear in mind that every action they take will directly affect the overall environment, in either positive or negative ways. She advised me to reduce my personal carbon footprint by cutting down on car emissions if I have access to public transport. She also gave me tips on saving energy as an essential way to put a stop to environmental degradation. Although we had just met, she was really helpful and friendly towards me, and I think that my talk with her was really informative.

MODEL SENTENCES FOR PAST EVENT DESCRIPTION

…..The occasion when I was angry was several months ago when I was about to board a flight at the airport…..

…..Our flight would be delayed due to the snowstorm/lightning/dense fog…..

…..The telephone conversation I would like to talk about is…..

…..At first, I felt extremely nervous since it was my first interview. I lacked confidence…..

…..During the conversation, however, I found the interviewer called Michael was fairly gentle and nice…..

…..Afterwards, I felt that she was satisfied with my performance…..

…..I started to skip class because I found it was boring…..

…..My mom was so happy that she decided to give me a surprise…..

…..I felt a sense of fulfillment. I was really impressed with my mother's special gift and it gave me a lasting memory…..

…..The wedding ceremony I would like to share with you is…..

…..Mike and I have been close friends since childhood. Therefore, when he invited me to be his best man, I agreed without any hesitation…..

…..We had a memorable and busy day back then…..

…..Before the ceremony, we had laboriously decorated and planned everything…..

…..It was one of the most unforgettable moments of my life…..

…..I was greatly frustrated and hopeless. I have never experienced something as difficult as that in my life…..

…..The exciting experience I would like to tell you about happened several years ago when I was a college student…..

…..There were two options for me which was whether to continue my study or to get a job right away. It was a really difficult choice that I had to make…..

…..I would like to talk about an occasion when I got up extremely early…..

…..I would like to tell you about the first paid job that I really enjoyed in my life…..

…..I really enjoy doing this work for some reasons….. the job gives me countless opportunities to improve my English skills…..

…..I learnt to swim when I was a small child because my parents believed that it would be useful for me…..

…..Swimming improves the health and helps me to avoid illness…..

…..I would like to tell you about a special meal on my 18th birthday party, which was cooked at home by my mother…..

…..For me, this was the most special meal in my life…..

…..I would like to tell you about the trip that I went on last summer, to the hometown of my classmate…..

…..I'm going to talk about my brother's wedding day, which took place several years ago in the town where I grew up…..

…..I would like to tell you about a situation that made me angry was getting stuck in a traffic jam…..

PART 3 SPEAKING INTRODUCTION

Remember that in part 1 speaking, the examiner will sit you down. They are going to check your ID, they are going to introduce themselves and they are going to ask you a series of questions in part 1 speaking about different topics. The first topic will either be *"do you work or study?"* or *"where are you living?"*, then it's followed up by two more topics; and those 2 topics could be about anything, but they won't be sensitive, and they won't be trick questions. Then you know that the examiner will move on part 2 speaking, and in part 2 speaking, they will give you a card, and they tell you that you have one minute to think about what you are going to say about the card, and you may take notes if you wish and you can use those notes while you are speaking. When you are done with your card in part 2 speaking, the examiner might ask you 2 follow-up questions. Those questions will be ridiculously simple, simpler than part 1 speaking questions. You are going to give a one-sentence answer, just answer the question, no need to extend. For example, if the examiner give you the card with the topic on it like *"Describe a place that your parent took you to"*, and when you are done with the card in part 2 speaking, then they might ask you 2 follow-up questions about the card like *"do you go to other places like this?"* and you just answer *"no, this is the only place that I have been to"* or if they ask you *"do your friends enjoy these kinds of places?"* and you just answer *"some friends of mine do, but most of them prefer something else"*. Just give a one-sentence answer.

Another example, if the examiner give you the card with the topic on it about a beautiful natural environment, they might ask you some follow-up questions like *"do you often go places like this?"* or *"which you recommend your friend go there?"* *"When was the last time you went to a place like this?"*

Just answer the question, no need to extent. If the examiner asks you follow-up questions, don't panic. It's not because you don't give it wrong. The examiner is simply trying to get more English from you.

Why are they asking you follow-up questions?

Again, they just want to get a little more English from you. That's it. Answer the questions and then stop.

Then what will happen? After the examiner ask you the follow-up questions, they are going to signal that they are moving to part 3 speaking. Part 3 speaking is a lot like part 1 speaking. Part 1 speaking involves questions that are simple, and they are about you, and other people. However, part 3 speaking questions are bigger questions, looking at bigger ideas, looking for your opinion, looking for your explanation. When I tell in your part 1 speaking that you should answer the question, and show something about your English ability. That's totally different from part 3 speaking. In part 3 speaking, the examiner wants you to answer the questions, but they also want you to have a lot more explanations. Your answers for part 3 questions should be 5-6 sentences long, NOT 1-2 sentences. The thing about part 3 speaking is simpler than part 1 is that the examiner will ask you questions, but here is **the difference**: in part 1 speaking, the examiner has the questions written down exactly. The questions will be in front of them, and they just ask you the questions exactly as they are written for part 1 speaking. The examiner is **not** allowed to change part 1 speaking questions, he must read as exactly what they are; no changes. If you ask him *"what the word means?"* in part 1 speaking, they are not going to answer, they just can repeat the question, but they cannot reword the question. They can't turn the question into different words so you could understand that more. For example, if the examiner ask you *"do you find foreign food delicious?"* and you don't know what *"delicious"* means, you can say *"what does "delicious" mean?"*, but they won't change the question for you. Overall, part 1 speaking questions are really quite easy, so you should not really have problems with like *"what do you mean by "how often"?* Well, if you don't know what *"how often"* means, that's a real problem. It's different from part 3 speaking. In part 3 speaking, the examiner **does not** have questions written down exactly in front of him, they just have basic ideas for the questions, and they will create the question for you based on how well you are doing in part 1 and part 2 speaking. In fact, by the time you are done with your part 2 speaking, the examiner has a very clear idea about what your band score is (5.0, 6.0, or 7.0+), so they will create the part 3 speaking questions based on how well you have done in part 1, and part 2 speaking. If you are about at 6.0 as they are feeling, they might ask you questions and words in a simpler way. If you are doing really well, they might ask you the same question but words in a more difficult way to invite a higher level in English from you. But here is what's important; in part 3 speaking if you don't understand the question, you can ask the examiner, and then they will *rephrase* the question in part 3 speaking so you could understand. For example, if they ask you *"what are the advantages of growing up in urban area?"* if you don't know what *"urban area"* means, you can ask them to rephrase the question, and then they will say *"what are the benefits of growing up in the city?"*. Certainly, they will reword it. **Do not** try to impress the examiner by answering the question you are not quite sure about. That's a problem. The examiner won't know if you lack the ability because you don't understand the question or you don't know how to communicate your answer. So, if you are not sure about the question, ask the examiner to rephrase. The examiner is going to create the questions in part 3 speaking. Also, the examiner is going to follow up your answers with questions. If the examiner says *"what are the benefits of growing up in the city?"*, and you say *"well, one of the huge advantages is being able to ride your motorbike around the city center"*, then they might ask you another questions *"what disadvantages of riding motorbikes in city areas?"* if you talk about motorbike, then they might start asking the question about motorbike.

Note that the topic for part 3 speaking will always be connected to part 2 speaking. So if they ask you to talk about a beautiful natural environment in part 2 speaking, part 3 speaking might be about the environment, might be about nature, might be about travel, and might be about pollution, whatever. If they give you a part 2 topic about something, you can think about what part 3 is going to be. The other thing about part 3 speaking is the questions are much broader. Part 3 speaking does require a lot more explanation, more opinions and they will require that you have some knowledge about things. This is where they start deciding if you can get a 7.0 because in part 3 speaking, you not only need to be influent and dramatically correct, but your answer needs to be very organized, and you need to be organized to over 5, 6 even 7 sentences, and you have to be prepared for the examiner to ask you follow-up questions that you might not expect.

Now, what is important in part 3 speaking? The important is that you do the best that you can in part 3 speaking to answer the question and to organize your answer. You don't need a lot of ideas. Part 3 speaking might involve questions about more academic topics. They might ask you about *"the environment"*, they might ask you about *"pollution"*, they might ask you about *"employment"* but you should not be under pressure to come up with some original brilliant ideas. One of the big things about part 3 speaking is more important than the huge range of grammar and vocabulary that is your **ORGANIZATION**. Organization is how you answer the question. Without organization, perfect grammar and vocabulary go out the window. You need organization if you want to get a high band score in speaking. I have a method here that works for part 3 speaking and task 2 writing and the method is the one I call the **"party scenario method"**. It's easy, let me show you how it works. This is what allows you to comfortably answer part 3 speaking questions. We will be working in details on the language that you need, but the basics. The basic thing that you need is what I am going to show you right now:

STEP 1: First of all, just answer the question. If you have problems with grammar, part 3 speaking is not the time for you to try using big vocabulary words that you don't know what they mean and long complicated sentences. If you have problems with grammar, you should be giving short sentences that are well linked. I am going to show you what I mean by this.

Let's try this *"should parents limit the amount of fast food their children eat?"*

Just like part 1 speaking question, don't forget to recognize that is an open or closed question. A lot of part 3 speaking questions will look like part 1 speaking questions. The only difference that the examiner wants more in part 3 speaking is they want you to have more explanations and more details.

So *"should parents limit the amount of fast food their children eat?"*

Step 1: Just answer the question

- *Yes, they should*

- *Yes, that's a good idea*

- *Yes, I think so*

- *Certainly, parents should limit the amount of fast food their children eat.*

- *Absolutely, parents should limit the amount of fast food their children eat.*

- *Yes, parents should limit the amount of fast food their children eat.*

STEP 2: Answer why do you think that? Note that <u>don't get too specific</u>; don't do what we call *"don't jump to conclusion"*

The benefit of the method *"party scenario"* is that if you just ask and answer some simple questions like *how, who, why, how often, what, when, where...simple, simple, simple, and simple detailed questions,* <u>you will be organizing your answer perfectly.</u> You shouldn't jump to the conclusion. <u>Start your answer in a general way,</u> then move towards specific.

+ What is the **1st** general reason why you think parents should limit the amount of fast food their children eat? What's wrong with fast food – give an <u>adjective</u> (unhealthy)

Yes, they should because it is <u>unhealthy</u>.

+ What is the **2nd** general reason? Why is it unhealthy?

It contains a lot of fat, calories, sugar, and high cholesterol.

+ What is the **3rd** general reason? Why are these things problems?

<u>As a result</u> (linking phrase), when children eat fast food too much, they may become overweight. In fact, it may lead to obesity.

+ What is the **4th** general reason? Why is obesity a problem?

<u>This may leads to</u> (linking phrase) serious diseases such as diabetes, cancer or heart diseases.

Why do we care about obesity?

Because it could cause obesity and heart disease. It may kill people.

+ What is the conclusion?

<u>Therefore</u> (linking phrase), it's a good idea for parents to make sure that their kids eat healthy food instead of fast food.

Well, all what I am doing here is that I am ending with a concluding statement. And what is my concluding statement? <u>A paraphrase of what</u>

I've said already. That works.

Overall, all I am doing to answer the question is that I am taking these simple sentences and I am linking them with phrases like *"as a result", "for example", "this may lead to"*. So, this is the general idea of what I organize here. It gets a little bit more complicated. However, I will say most of what we have learnt for part 1 speaking is going to serve you here. You are going to need comparisons, types of people, these kinds of adjectives *(healthy, unhealthy,..)* Let me tell you that being organized this way will help you overcome your grammar problems. Organization overcomes grammar, and the good news is this is exactly the same method that you are going to need for task 2 writing. Answer the question, and then give the examiner an explanation.

Example: *what are the advantages of studying abroad?*

Better education (great facilities like libraries, laboratory, and comfortable dormitory) – why are they helpful? (To prepare people for the future careers)

Answer: *there are a lot of advantages when studying abroad, for example, they offer better facilities. To be specific, the university offers high tech laboratory, modern library…as a result, students may be better prepared for their future career.*

Example: *what kind of gifts do people typically give in your country?*

Answer: *We give presents for different national holidays. To be specific, during this national holiday (Mid-autumn festival), boys and girls usually give their parents, grandparents X (flowers and cakes). However, in this holiday (Lunar New Year) at the end of the year, parents give their children lucky money. On the other hand/meanwhile, we may give presents for private celebrations such as birthday, wedding or even graduation party.*

Nice, well-organized answer and your sentences are short. In addition, I'm linking those sentences with certain phrases such as *"for example", "to be specific", "as a result", "this may lead to", "however", "on the other hand/meanwhile"*. Remember, you must have the main idea before explaining.

So, what we have here is a range of questions, and some of them do look a lot like part 1 speaking. However, understand that in part 3 speaking, the examiner wants more explanation, they want more comparison, and you are going to use the same structures that you use in part 1 speaking so you could build your answer.

LANGUAGE FOR GIVING AND SUPPORTING OPINIONS

To express your opinions like a native, you must:

1. Introduce and give your opinions clearly.
2. Support your opinions with reasons or examples.

It's very easy to learn a variety of different ways to express your opinion when being asked a question. Look at these examples:

I think that *(I think that Apple makes the best phone.)*

I don't think that *(I don't think that public transport should be free of charge.)*

I believe that *(I believe that this business will be profitable.)*

I don't believe that *(I don't believe that people can be persistent and productive if they don't like what they do.)*

I am convinced that *(I am convinced that parents should limit the amount of fast food that their children eat)*

As far as I am concerned *(As far as I am concerned, parents should limit the amount of fast food that their children eat)*

When it comes to native speaker expressions for giving and supporting opinions, I want you to be thinking about 2 things: one is that I want you to keep it simple. The language that I gave you above is meant to supplement your ideas, but it will not replace your ideas, and it will not replace your organization as well. The other thing I want you to be always thinking about and remember is the **"party scenario method"**, you should always be asking simple follow-up questions.

Should people use public transportation?

Yes, I think they should mainly because the traffic here is so dangerous for example the traffic jam can cause impolite behaviors and because some people don't follow the rules, then that causes a lot of collisions. As a result,…..

To support your opinion, you can also use **common sense language**, **general statistics**, or **expert and opinions** in your speaking.

COMMON SENSE LANGUAGE:

- *Everyone knows that fast food is unhealthy.*
- *Everyone knows that you should wear a helmet when you ride a motorbike.*
- *Everyone knows that driving a car without a seat belt is very dangerous.*
- *It's common knowledge that fast food can cause obesity.*
- *It's common knowledge that obesity may lead to diabetes.*

GENERAL STATISTICS:

- *Thousands of people suffer from diabetes.*
- *Increasing numbers of people who suffer from diabetes.*
- *The number of people who suffer from diabetes is growing.*
- *There are thousands of chemicals in fast food*
- *There are hundreds of ways that fast food can kill you*

EXPERT AND OPINIONS

- *According to doctors,….*
- *According to researchers,…..*
- *According to the latest research,….*
- *According to medical studies,…..*
- *According to what I saw in the news last night,……*

- *According to* what I read in the newspaper last week,…..
- *According to* what my uncle told me,……

PRACTICE QUESTIONS

1. Do you think the Internet should be censored?

2. What do you think about governments investing money in space travel?

3. Is city life suitable for children?

4. Are films showing too much sex and violence these days?

5. Should people be concerned about the increasing population?

6. Has fast food had any positive effects on society?

7. Do you feel parents should limit their children's time spent using technology?

8. Do celebrities make too much money?

9. Should teenagers have to learn life skills such as sewing, cooking, and basic repairs in school?

10. Is it a good idea for governments to issue heavy fines to people who litter?

TALKING ABOUT ADVANTAGES AND DISADVANTAGES

The nice thing about advantages and disadvantages questions is the fact that you can change a lot of part 3 speaking questions into advantages and disadvantages questions.

Example: *Should parents limit the amount of fast food their children eat?*

You can say: *Yes, they should because fast food has a lot of disadvantages.*

Great, you have just switched the question into disadvantages question.

Moreover, this kind of language is something that comes up in task 2 writing.

Example: *What are the advantages and disadvantages of buying and using a motor car?*

Answer order:

1. Use introducing advantages phrases:

One of the main advantages of X is….

One of the main benefits of X is….

Another good thing about X is…..

One more great thing about X is…

Example:

One of the main benefits/ advantages of owning a car is that it is convenient *(long distance travel)*

Another good thing about owning a car is weather protection.

One more great thing about car ownership is time-consuming/ save a lot of time compared to public transportation/ carry more people.

2. Then you simply signal something like *"in contrast/ however/ on the other hand"* and tell the listener that you have done talking about the advantages, now you are talking about the disadvantages.

The main disadvantage of X is: *The main disadvantage of living in a modern city is the noise.* (About the environment)

One drawback of X is: *One drawback of owning a car is that it's very expensive.* (About finance)

One disadvantage of X is: *One disadvantage of owning a car is being able to find a parking space in major cities.*

"A car offers a lot of conveniences, but it can be inconvenient too."

"Although a car is very convenient, sometimes it's very inconvenient."

"It can be a great convenience to own a car. However*, it can be inconvenient, for example, in many cities, owing a car could cause you to get stuck in the traffic jam because cars are* not as moveable as *motorbikes.* Moreover*, trend to find parking can be a problem because there are not a lot of areas for car parking in major cities."*

"Although cars show people how rich you are, they do cost a lot of money (taxes, gas, parking, services...)"

Does fast food have any positive effect on society?

You could say: *Yes, it does. One of the advantages of fast food is that it is very convenient.*

How? Now you need to explain how it is convenient.

What I mean is when people are very busy, they can stop somewhere and get something delicious to eat, and it doesn't take very long.......

Some good language here: **concession & contrast.**

- Something is true at the same time something else is true.
- Something is true. However, something else is true.
- Although this is true, that is true.

Example:

Men <u>tend to</u> do some strenuous sports like football or basketball; however, women <u>are more likely to</u> be interested in aerobic exercises like yoga...

Elderly people <u>are more likely to</u> shop at open markets, or second-hand markets. They love buying stuff on sale and bargaining; however, young guys <u>tend to</u> shop at big shopping malls, department stores and fancy boutiques.

HYPOTHETICALS

Hypotheticals are very important when it comes to part 1 and part 2 speaking. When they give you a hypothetical question, they are signaling that they want a certain kind of answer. They are signaling that they want a certain type of grammar here. That's very important that we understand hypotheticals.

What is a hypothetical?

A hypothetical is <u>an imaginary situation</u>. If we are talking about the future, it's an imaginary situation. What you need to pay attention to hypotheticals will be <u>dealing with the modal verbs</u> "would/could/should". You might hear these questions in part 1 speaking "would/could/should" like *"would you ever ride your motorbike without your helmet?"* It is a hypothetical question.

You even might get <u>hypothetical questions in the past</u>.

How do we use hypothetical questions in the past?

We talk about things that we would do. When we talk about things that we would do, we need to signal that we are talking about things in the past; and you're talking about things that you did a lot in the past. For example, you might say:

I had a lot of fun when I was a kid. My friends and I would often go to the beach, and sometimes we played football. Occasionally, we would go to the movie.

So what I am saying *"we would often go to the beach"*; *"we would go to the movie"*

I'm using the same modal verbs that I am using for the future tense, but I'm using them in the past. I'm signaling that I am talking in the past. It's a very useful grammar structure because you are talking with the examiner about things that you did a lot in the past.

When it comes to the part 2 speaking, if the examiner gives you a hypothetical question, they are going to ask you to talk about the future.

Do you live in an apartment or a house?

I live in an apartment. Is this a good answer? Of course, **not**.

What should you say?

I live in a big apartment with three classmates on the corner of.... (much better).

I've been living in a big apartment with three friends on the corner of....

Which is the best room?

My favorite room is living room. I like it _more than_ my bedroom. There is a television in the living room, so I am _a lot less bored_ when I spend time there (comparison).

What _would_ you like to change? (Pay attention to the modal "would")

I would change the color of my walls

I'd paint my walls

I'd build a bookshelf.

I'd buy a big Television.

PRACTICE QUESTIONS

1. What are the advantages of owning and using a car? What are the disadvantages?

2. What are some of the advantages and disadvantages of using social media websites?

3. Tell me about the disadvantages of city life?

4. Compare the advantages of working from home with the disadvantages

5. What are some disadvantages of studying abroad?

6. What are the advantages of travelling alone? What are the disadvantages?

7. What are some of the advantages and disadvantages of using the Internet for completing homework?

PROPOSING SOLUTIONS TO PROBLEM

If the examiner ask you a question about problems, they are **not** going to ask you questions about your personal problem. Instead, they will ask you questions about problems in your hometown, or problems in people's everyday lives. They are not going to ask you questions about your personal problems. They are **not** asking you like *"have you ever broken up with a girlfriend or a boyfriend." "Are your parents divorced?"* But they might ask you something like *"Why do friendships break up?"*

The kinds of problems we are talking about might be the environment, education, crime, unemployment, transportation, etc.

The questions may take many forms. They might ask you about problems and solutions. Or they might ask you about problems, then you answer blah..blah..blah.., and then they will ask you about solutions, they could break it up, they might even ask you just something about solutions because understand if they ask you questions about the disadvantages of whatever, for example *the disadvantages of owning a car*, and you start talking about problems, they might ask you some follow up questions about what you just said *"what are solutions to these problems you are talking about?"*

It doesn't matter because like I said, what you need to say is really quite clear.

If they ask you questions about problems *"what types of environmental problems exist in your country?"*

Answer order:

1. First of all, answer the question by identifying the problem or problems *"air pollution and water pollution"*
2. Explain the causes *"where does the pollution come from?", "why do we have pollution?"*
   ...due to private vehicles, factories, loss of trees.
3. Talk about the effects of these causes (very important). You should tell the examiner *"why we should care?", "why is this a problem?"*
4. Suggest solutions.

5. Suggest definite actions that should be taken.

Language to identify problems:

One major concern with the environment that needs addressing is air pollution.

The biggest problem with the environment is air pollution.

The main issue many people have with the environment is air pollution.

Most people believe that air problem *is the main problem.*

Language to explain causes:

The main reasons behind **this** (paraphrasing for air pollution)

The main reasons behind **this** *are too many private vehicles in the city as well as the rise of factories since my country has become a manufacturing country.*

The main reason behind **this** *is the increase production from factories to meet customers' demands.*

This (paraphrasing for air pollution) *is caused by Y and Z.*

This (paraphrasing for air pollution) *is caused as a result of Y and Z.*

Language to explain effects:

This pollution leads to global warming in a long term this is because....

As a result of this, global warming and health issues have increased.

Language to suggest solutions:

You need to tell the examiner:

1. Who should do something? and be specific. Don't just say *"people"*, instead you should say *"governments", "teachers", "students", "teenagers", etc.* you don't have to be so specific, try to be <u>a little bit specific</u>. Remember, you should use modal verbs (people <u>should</u>, government <u>ought to</u>, businesses <u>need to</u>/<u>must</u>/<u>could</u>; they <u>should</u> be encouraged to)

2. What should they do? Give the examiner some explanations, and then your prediction *(if the government invest in public transportation, then I think it's very probable that pollution level will have decreased in the next 20 years)*
3. Why do you think these solutions will work?

When it comes to the language of *"problem/solution"*, something you should pay attention to is the fact you have some really good verbs here: *<u>could</u> spend more money on/ <u>should</u> spend more money on/ <u>ought to</u> spend more money on/ <u>can</u> spend more money on.*

My point is you should be using *"could/ should/ ought to/ can/ must/ need to"* to talk about "solutions". We have an example here:

COULD/ SHOULD/ OUGHT TO/ CAN/ MUST/ NEED TO + VERB/ PHRASE

- *People should use more public transportation*
- *Corporations <u>ought to take steps to</u> reduce their emissions*
- *Governments can <u>provide incentives</u> for people who use public transportation.*
- *The government could <u>make an effort to</u> reduce taxes for people who use public transportation.*
- *In my opinion, the government <u>ought to take steps to</u> improve the public transportation.*
- *In my opinion, parents <u>ought to take steps to</u> teach their children how to do homework.*
- *Teachers ought to <u>provide tips</u> for studying.*
- *Parents ought to <u>provide instructions on how to</u> budget their children's money.*
- *The government ought to <u>provide health insurance for people</u> who don't have a lot of money.*
- *The police need to <u>take steps to solve the problem</u>.*
- *We should <u>pay more attention to</u> eat healthy food.*
- *Parents should <u>take measures to</u> teach their children about cycling.*

BY + VERB-ING

- *The government could improve the situation <u>by imposing</u> tighter regulations on…*

- *The government could improve things <u>by cleaning up</u> the most polluted areas of...*
- *We could fix this problem <u>by putting</u> pressure on local governments to...*
- *We could take measures to solve this problem <u>by spending</u> more money on education and less on arms...*
- *We can make it a lot better <u>by repairing</u> the damage and by renovating the building...*

<u>Example:</u> **What type of education problems does your country face?**

Lack of quality – what are the causes of "lack of quality" -- lack of funding.

Less practical experience/skills – therefore, when they attend university, they might not be as prepared as students from other countries.

These are very good structures: <u>comparisons, conditionals, cause and effect language</u> and linking them together is the series of simple things that makes a good answer.

<u>Example:</u> **What are problems with children who idolize celebrities?**

Well, <u>one major concern with worshipping famous</u> people that needs addressing is children may develop the bad habits of their idols. <u>What I mean is</u> children might watch their favorite movie stars drinking alcohol or smoking cigarettes, and then the child try these behaviors themselves. <u>The main reasons behind this are that</u> children know that people admire celebrities, so they feel like they will be worshipped if they smoke cigarettes and drink beer just like celebrities do. This can cause a lot of problems. <u>This situation can lead children to</u> become criminals or maybe lose the respects of their friends and family. <u>As a result,</u> they don't spend so much time in the library like they used to. It's difficult to get children to want to read. One thing that parents could do that they can give their son and daughter a little bit of money every time they read a book....

This is a good answer because I have just said something about the problem. What are the effects of the problem? And the very simple solutions that involve who should do something, and what they should do?

PRACTICE QUESTIONS

1. What types of education problems does your country face? Can you suggest any solutions?

2. What challenges does a young married couple typically deal with?

3. What are the drawbacks of living in the countryside?

4. What problems with the environment does your country face? What do you propose done to reduce the problems?

5. What solutions can you suggest to lower crime rates in big cities?

6. Are there any problems with children idolizing celebrities?

7. How does using electronic gadgets hurt relationships? Can anything be done to improve this situation?

8. How can we get children to read more books?

9. Do farmers in your country face any major challenges? What are they?

AGREEING AND DISAGREEING

The examiner will give you questions about your OPINION, not a ~~FACT~~ and then they will ask you *"do you agree with this opinion?"*

They **won't** ask you questions like *"Japan is in Asia. How much do you agree with that?", "I have a sandwich for lunch. Do you agree or disagree?"*

These questions <u>must be opinions</u>. They cannot ask you agree or disagree with a fact. It doesn't make sense if they give you a fact.

Of course, when they ask you *"do you agree?"* Or *"do you disagree?"*

What kind of question they are asking you? Open or closed question? Definitely <u>closed question</u>. And the first thing you will do is to answer the question:

- *Yes, I agree*
- *No, I disagree*

So that is the first thing you need to think about it. Go back to part 1 speaking, answer *"yes/no"* to show your answer to the question.

Is it ok for us to say that we <u>kind of agree</u> but we also <u>kind of disagree</u>?

Definitely **yes**, and you could use phrases like this:

PARTIAL DISAGREEMENT PHRASES:

I can see your point, but…(<u>talk about what you disagree with</u>)

I agree with that up to a point, but….(I disagree with other things -- <u>talk about what you disagree with</u>).

I kind of agree with that…(I disagree with other things -- <u>talk about what you disagree with</u>).

You can just give them <u>a basic general statement</u> like *"well, I agree with some points of that, but some points of that I disagree with"*

So, what is really important here is that you are giving a clear first opinion so the examiner could know what you are talking about. Are you talking about <u>one side</u> (agree or disagree) or are you talking about <u>both sides</u> (agree and disagree). It makes a big difference because you may have grammar problem, vocabulary problem and pronunciation problem; but if your answer is not clear right away, the examiner is really having a hard time figuring out *"what are you answering?", "Will you be explaining something?"* because your main idea is not clear.

TOTAL DISAGREEMENT PHRASES:

Honestly, I <u>absolutely disagree</u> with you because…

Honestly, I <u>totally disagree</u> with you because…

<u>I'm afraid that I disagree</u> with you because…

I'm sorry, but I <u>can't possibly agree</u> with that because…

The reason why you agree and disagree with these phrases are you can talking about *cause and effect* logic.

<u>For example:</u> *I hate iPhones because they are expensive and have a short battery life. <u>As a result/ therefore</u>, I prefer Samsung.*

You can talk about *cause and effect* in multiple ways here:

Eating fast food <u>leads to</u> diabetes.

A lot of children eat fast food. <u>As a result</u>, this leads them to have obesity.

LANGUAGE FOR EXPRESSING LIKELIHOOD

Certain, fairly certain, or uncertain.

Certain: I would say this does not mean 100%; it's about 80%, 90%. *(It's quite likely/ highly likely/ very likely/ extremely likely.)*

Fairly certain: *it is likely/ probable/ possible.*

Uncertain: *it's quite unlikely/ highly unlikely/ very unlikely/ extremely unlikely.*

THE FUTURE PERFECT & THE FUTURE CONTINUOUS

THE FUTURE PERFECT STRUCTURE: WILL + HAVE + PAST PARTICIPLE

By next week, I <u>will have taken</u> the IELTS.

By next week, I <u>will have sold</u> my bike.

By next week, I <u>will have climbed</u> the mountain.

All of them are <u>finished actions by a certain time in the future</u>. In order to use the future perfect, you will need Will + have + past participle + a time. We can't have a finished action in the future if we don't tell when we finish. So you need to be able to say *"I will have climbed the mountain by next Saturday."* Or *"I will have taken the exam by Tuesday."*

THE FUTURE CONTINUOUS STRUCTURE: WILL + BE + V-ING

Future continuous is <u>an action in progress in the future</u>.

By next Saturday, I will be climbing a mountain.

By next week, I will be taking the IELTS exam.

<u>Example:</u> ***How will the transportation develop in your city in the next 10 years?***

How do you produce your main idea?

Your main idea is going to be this: *<u>Given that</u> they have started building the train in the middle of the city. <u>I think it is very likely</u> that a train will have been built in the next decade.*

And now you are going to <u>explain</u> by using maybe <u>conditionals, cause and effect</u>…

"What I mean is we have a lot of pollution in my city and one way to reduce this is to build more public transportation. So, the government has invested in the train and they are planning to finish in the next 10 years."

Explain by giving some details about *"why we need a train?", "who would use the train?", "what the effect will be?",*

You can make prediction: *in my opinion, I believe the train is going to be very popular. I think <u>it's extremely likely</u> that <u>fewer people</u> ride motorbikes, and <u>more people</u> will be taking the train.*

<u>Example:</u> **Will robots become common in people's lives in the future?**

<u>Given that</u>, *people are so busy at the job these days. I think <u>it's highly probable that</u> people will have a robot to help their everyday needs. For example, housewives who have to take care of their children and might have a part time job, they could use a robot to help clean house or send the robot to the market to buy vegetables, and I think this is very helpful and I hope that I will have a robot of my own someday. I would really like one.*

PRACTICE QUESTIONS

1. Will people live on another planet someday in your lifetime?

2. In your lifetime, will there be any significant changes to the way people travel?

3. Do you think going to the cinema will be more or less popular in the future?

4. Do you think the traditional duties of men and women will change in the future?

5. In the next few decades, do you think traditional food in your country will change?

6. How do you think technology will affect education in the future?

7. What effect will Facebook and Twitter have on cultural exchange as increasing numbers of people in the world use the Internet?

8. What role might environmental problems play in where people live in the future?

9. What do you think city life will be like in the future? Will the countryside change?

10. Do you think it is likely that robots will replace humans in common tasks in your lifetime?

MODEL SENTENCES FOR PART 3 SPEAKING

What are the differences between X and Y?

Answer structure: *Well, although they look quite similar and they do share a lot in common, there are many significant differences between them. For example, X is…..while Y is……. Another difference is that X is…….However, Y is…....Besides,……*

What are the differences between a lawyer and a police officer?

Well, although they look quite similar and they do share a lot in common, there are many significant differences between them. For example, a lawyer is someone whose job is to advise people about laws, or represent people in court, while a police officer is someone who works for an official organization and their job is to catch criminals and make sure that people obey the law. Another difference is that their looks are quite different as well. A lawyer normally wears a decent suit or a smart dress; however, a police officer usually wears a police uniform and looks really cool. Besides, a lawyer is more quick-responsive, logical and articulate while a police officer has to be physically strong and mentally agile.

What do you think a good…should be like?

Answer structure: *I think it takes a lot of things to…. For example,…should be…It is very hard to imagine how someone can be a good …without …Another qualification a good……should have is …the most important thing is that, a good …has to be …*

What do you think a good teacher should be like?

I think it takes a lot of things to be a good teacher. For example, a good teacher should be responsible. It is very hard to imagine how someone can be a good teacher without a certain responsibility. Another qualification a good teacher should have is knowledgeable. The most important thing is that, a good teacher has to be inspiring. I mean, they should encourage and inspire students to show their initiative to learn rather than force them to study….

PART 3 SPEAKING QUESTIONS FOR PRACTICE

FRIENDSHIP

- Is it easy to make friends?
- What is the most important thing when you make friends?
- What is the importance of friendship?
- What should a real friend be like?
- Do people love to make friends with youngster or the elderly people?
- Is it possible for people to have friends of different ages? Explain why.
- What do you usually say when you meet someone for the first time?
- Where and when do you usually meet your friends?
- How do computer and mobile phone affect friendship?
- Do you think common interest is important in making friends?
- Do you have any foreign friends?
- Where can you meet foreigners in your hometown?
- Where and when do you usually hang out with foreign friends?
- What do you usually do when you hang out with foreign friends?
- Do you have difficulties when you talk about culture with foreigners?
- Do you think the immigration may affect another country?

SUCCESSFUL PEOPLE

- What do you think a successful person should be like?

- What qualities do you think a successful person should have?

- How to become a successful leader?

- How to become a leader?

- How to become a star?

- Are there any differences between a successful person and a celebrity?

- What are the disadvantages of being a celebrity?

- Do you think celebrities deserve being paid so much money?

- Do you want to become a celebrity? Why or why not?

- Who is your idol? Can you give some names of the idols? Why do you love them?

- Do you want to become a person like that? How to become a person like that?

ADVERTISEMENT

- How do you feel about advertisements?
- What are the different types of advertisements?
- What are the functions and the problems of advertisements?
- What are the effects that advertisements have on people?
- How do you feel about the celebrities endorse the big brands?
- How do you feel about those false advertisements?
- What influences do false advertisements have on people?
- Are you going to be tempted into buying something you don't actually need by advertisements?
- What do you think of people are splashing out on the luxurious stuff?
- What should a good advertisement be like?
- What kind of advertisement attracts people most?
- Do you think there are too many advertisements nowadays?
- Should government restrict the advertisements?
- Do you think it is good if children advertise the product?
- Why are those people who advertise products always good-looking?
- & Why do companies always invite celebrities in the advertisements?

TEACHING

- Do you think teaching is a very important job?

- What qualifications does a great teacher should have?

- Please talk about the advantages and disadvantages of being a teacher?

- Do you think teachers are well-paid in your country?

- How to improve the teachers' social status?

- What's the difference between teachers past and now?

- What are the differences between public schools and private schools?

- What are the differences of education compare the old days with today?

- Which way do you prefer to study, self-study or having lectures?

ADVICE

- What do your parents tell you about the things you should do and shouldn't do in school?

- Do children listen to their parents' advice?

- What do you think of peer pressure?

- Should a successful person be able to make his own decision or listen to others' advice?

- Would you make decision based on others' advice?

ADVENTUROUS PEOPLE

- What do you think an adventurous person should be like?

- What are the differences between adventurous and reckless?

- Which kind of people do you like more, adventurous people or cautious people?

ANIMALS

- What is your favourite animal?

- What do you think of pets?

- Do you think pets are faithful to their owners?

- What do you think caused the serious wildlife extinction?

- What do you think of the ecological environment?

- What do you think of the ecosystem?

- What kind of laws do you think governments should enact to prevent more endangered species from extinction?

- Does the law on the wildlife protection need to be improved further?

CELL PHONES

- Do you love cell phones?
- How often do you usually use cell phones?
- Whom do you usually call?
- What kind of stuff do you guys usually talk on the phone?
- Do you enjoy a long talk over the phone with your buddies?
- Have cell phones become a "must-have" for people today?
- Which ones do you prefer, cell phones or landlines?
- Why do you think students are forbidden to use cell phones at school?
- Are cell phones influencing the students' school life? In what way?

COMPUTERS

- How do you feel about computers?

- What influence do you think computers have on kids?

- Which ones do you prefer, desktops or laptops?

- What are the differences between desktops and laptops?

- Which brand of the laptops do you prefer? Why?

- How often do you usually surf the internet?

- Generally speaking, how long do you surf the internet every day?

FASHION & SHOPPING

- How do you feel about fashion?

- Do you think different people have different opinions about fashion? Why?

- In terms of fashion, do you think only those internationally famous brands are the latest fashions?

- Do you like shopping? Why or why not?

- Where and when do you usually go shopping?

- Do you like to go shopping alone or with friends?

- Where do you usually like to go shopping, online or big shopping malls?

- Do you think online shopping will replace the shopping malls some day?

- What are the disadvantages of online shopping?

- How to improve these disadvantages of online shopping?

- Why the prices of the goods in big shopping malls are much higher than the prices of goods online?

- Why do you think girls like windowing shopping? Don't you think it is a waste of time and energy?

- What are the differences comparing the clothes the elderly people wear with the clothes the youngsters wear? What are the differences of shopping habits comparing elderly people and young guys today?

- What kind of clothes do you like to wear on different occasions?

- What colors do you love most when you choose clothes?

- Which is more important when you choose clothes, the quality, the design, the pattern or the price? Why?

- Do you think we can judge people by what they wear?

- Do you think we can judge people by the colour of the clothes they wear?

- What role do you think clothes play in your life?

GIFTS

- When do you usually send others gifts?

- What do you usually send others as gifts?

- When do people in your country usually send gifts to each other?

- Are festivals the only occasion when people usually send gifts to each other?

- Are there any special rules or customs when people select gifts?

- Why do you think people always send gifts on some occasions? What is it for?

- What gifts did you usually get?

- From whom did you usually get gifts?

- When did you usually get gifts?

- What kinds of gifts do elderly people and little kids prefer?

TRANSPORTATION

- What are the popular public transports in your country?
- What are the things you don't love about transport in your country?
- What do you think causes the serious traffic problems?
- Since there are some problems involved in transport in your country, how do you think these problems can be solved?
- How do you feel about the future of the public traffic system in your country?
- How do people go to work in your city?
- How do you go to school or work every day?
- What do you think the public transportations in the future would be like?
- What differences between taxis and private cars?
- What are the advantages of riding bicycles?

PHOTOGRAPHY

- How can people take good photos?

- Do you like taking pictures or taking pictures of you?

- How do you feel about being a professional photography?

- How do you feel about photography?

- What are the difference between a photographer and a painter?

- How to become a professional photographer?

- Which ones would you prefer, traditional cameras or digital ones? Why?

- What kind of pictures do you love taking?

- When do people usually take photos?

- What are the differences between photos and videotapes?

- What are the differences between photographers and cameramen?

MUSIC

- Do you love music?
- What kind of music do you love?
- Why do you think different guys love totally different kinds of music?
- What kind of instrument do you love? Why?
- Have you ever learned to play any instrument before?
- What is the importance of learning to play different instruments?
- What are the differences compare the western music and your country music?
- What kind of music do you think young guys today prefer? Why?

FILMS

- Where do you usually watch films, at home or at the cinema?

- In what way do you think a cinema can attract more people?

- What do you think of those films with those special effects?

- Where do you usually get news, TV, magazines, newspapers or internet?

- What do you think a highly qualified journalist should be like?

- Are there any things that photographers, journalists and the cameramen share in common?

SPORTS

- Do you love doing sports?

- What kinds of sports do you love doing?

- What are the differences of favourite sports compare women and men?

- What are the differences of favourite sports compare the elderly people and youngsters?

- What kinds of sports do kids in your country like to play?

- What are the differences erf people's favourite sports compare before and today?

- Which way do you prefer to enjoy matches, watch by TV or actually be a part of the match?

FOOD

- What kind of food do Chinese love?
- What are the differences of the favourite food compare the elderly people with young guys?
- What are the differences of the favourite food compare old days with today?
- What are the differences of the favourite food compare women and men?
- What are the differences between western food and eastern food?
- Why are there more and more people dying to eat out rather than at home?
- Where do you like to eat, five-star restaurant or a small street restaurant?
- What do you usually consider when you choose a restaurant?
- How do you think a restaurant can attract more customers?
- Do you love to try food that you have never tried before?
- Can you name any food unhealthy? Why?
- What is the relation between food and health?
- What should a country do about food to improve citizens' health?
- What diseases can a certain kind of food cause?

TV PROGRAMMES

- What are the differences compare the TV programmes in old days and today?

- What are the differences compare the TV programmes women like and men like?

- What are the differences compare the TV programmes the elderly people like and youngsters like?

- Do you like watching TV?

- What kind of TV programmes do you like watching?

RELAXATION

- How do you like to relax?
- What do you usually do at night?
- What do you usually do at weekends?
- Do you like to have fun alone or hang out with your friends?
- What kinds of relaxation methods are popular?
- What are the differences compare the way people get relaxed before and now?
- What are the differences compare the way women get relaxed and men get relaxed?
- Do you think people should work at weekends?
- Do you think people who are working at weekends should get double paid?

NEWSPAPERS AND MAGAZINES

- What are the differences between newspapers and magazines?

- What are the differences between magazines and TVs?

- What are the differences compare the magazines today and in the past?

- What are the differences compare the magazines that women like and men like?

- What are the differences compare the magazines the elderly people like and youngster love?

- Which ones do you love more, international newspapers or local newspapers?

PARTIES

- Do you like parties?

- How often do you usually hang out?

- Do you like a small get-together or a big party?

- What do you usually do when you party?

- Besides singing karaoke and eating out, what else do you do at parties?

- What is your poison/your favourite drink?

- What are the differences between formal parties and informal ones?

- What are the differences compare the parties with friends with the one with family members?

- Where do you usually hold party, at home or somewhere else?

TRAVELLING

- Which way do you prefer to travel, by group or alone?
- What are the advantages and disadvantages of traveling by group or travel agencies?
- What are the advantages and disadvantages of traveling alone?
- How do you feel about the backpacking?
- What can you get by traveling? What is the importance of traveling?
- What are the advantages and disadvantages of tourism industry?
- How can a place benefit from the local tourism industry?
- How can government encourage and sponsor the local tourism industry?
- How can a place attract more tourists to visit?
- How do you feel about the development of tourism in your country?
- Do you think the advantages of tourism development outweigh the disadvantages? Why?
- Do you think overdevelopment of tourism industry caused too much pollution?
- Are there any good solutions to improve this situation?

NOISE

- Do you want to travel around the world?

- What is the cause of noise?

- How do you feel about noise?

- What consequences will noise cause?

- How to reduce noise?

- Are there any good solutions that government and individuals should do to deal with it?

- Besides noise pollution, is that any other kinds of pollution you think is very severe in your country?

READING

- Do people in your country love reading books?
- What kinds of book do they like reading?
- What kinds of books are popular in your country?
- Do you love reading books or novels online?
- Do you think online books will replace the real books some day?
- Are you into reading those academic books, text books and reference books?

FESTIVALS

- How do people in your country celebrate the festivals?

- What do people usually do on festivals?

- What are the differences compare the way people celebrated the festivals in the past with today?

- How do you feel about the festivals in your country?

- How do you like the western festivals? Can you name some of the western festivals are getting widespread in your country?

- What should the government do to remain the traditional festivals' features and signatures? •

- Can you name some of the tradition-featured festivals? And tell me what people usually do in these festivals?

PARKS

- How often do you usually go to parks?

- What influence do you think parks have on people's life?

- What kinds of people like to go to parks?

- What do people usually do in parks?

- Do people usually go for a walk, walk dogs and birds in the park?

CONCLUSION

Thank you again for downloading this book on *"IELTS Speaking Strategies: The Ultimate Guide with Tips, Tricks and Practice on How to Get a Target Band Score of 8.0+ in 10 Minutes a Day."* and reading all the way to the end. I'm extremely grateful.

If you know of anyone else who may benefit from the useful strategies, structures, tips, Part 1 + Part 2 + Part 3 Speaking language in this book, please help me inform them of this book. I would greatly appreciate it.

Finally, if you enjoyed this book and feel that it has added value to your work and study in any way, please take a couple of minutes to share your thoughts and post a REVIEW on Amazon. Your feedback will help me to continue to write other books of IELTS topic that helps you get the best results. Furthermore, if you write a simple REVIEW with positive words for this book on Amazon, you can help hundreds or perhaps thousands of other readers who may want to improve their English speaking sounding like a native speaker. Like you, they worked hard for every penny they spend on books. With the information and recommendation you provide, they would be more likely to take action right away. We really look forward to reading your review.

Thanks again for your support and good luck!

If you enjoy my book, please write a POSITIVE REVIEW on Amazon.

-- Rachel Mitchell --

CHECK OUT OTHER BOOKS

Go here to check out other related books that might interest you:

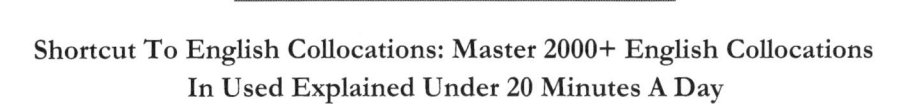

Shortcut To English Collocations: Master 2000+ English Collocations In Used Explained Under 20 Minutes A Day

https://www.amazon.com/dp/B06W2P6S22

IELTS Writing Task 1 + 2: The Ultimate Guide with Practice to Get a Target Band Score of 8.0+ In 10 Minutes a Day

https://www.amazon.com/dp/B075DFYPG6

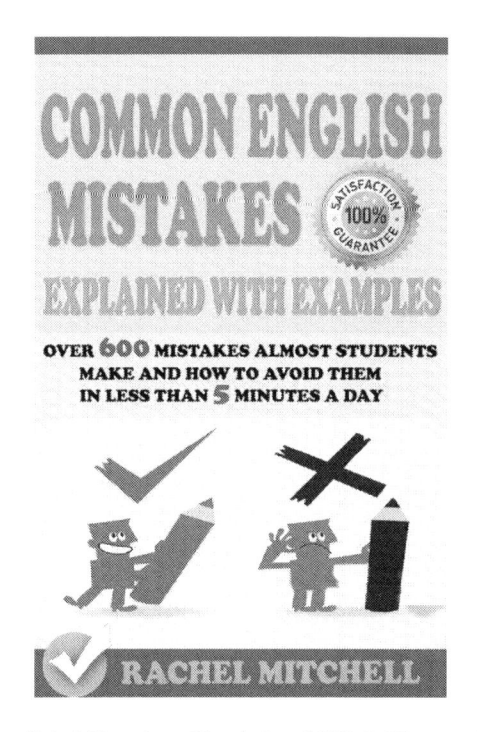

Common English Mistakes Explained With Examples: Over 600 Mistakes Almost Students Make and How to Avoid Them in Less Than 5 Minutes A Day

https://www.amazon.com/dp/B072PXVHNZ

Paraphrasing Strategies: 10 Simple Techniques For Effective Paraphrasing In 5 Minutes Or Less

https://www.amazon.com/dp/B071DFG27Q

Legal Vocabulary In Use: Master 600+ Essential Legal Terms And
Phrases Explained In 10 Minutes A Day

http://www.amazon.com/dp/B01L0FKXPU

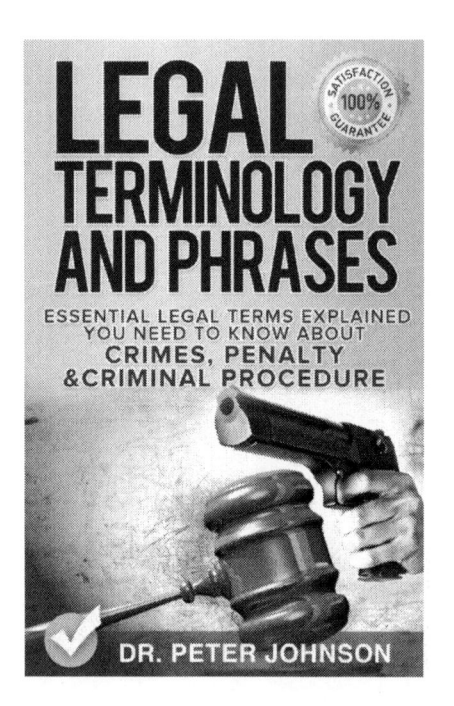

Legal Terminology And Phrases: Essential Legal Terms Explained You Need To Know About Crimes, Penalty And Criminal Procedure

http://www.amazon.com/dp/B01L5EB54Y

Productivity Secrets For Students: The Ultimate Guide To Improve Your Mental Concentration, Kill Procrastination, Boost Memory And Maximize Productivity In Study

http://www.amazon.com/dp/B01JS52UT6

Daughter of Strife: 7 Techniques On How To Win Back Your Stubborn Teenage Daughter

https://www.amazon.com/dp/B01HS5E3V6

Parenting Teens With Love And Logic: A Survival Guide To Overcoming The Barriers Of Adolescence About Dating, Sex And Substance Abuse

https://www.amazon.com/dp/B01JQUTNPM

Understanding Men in Relationships: The Top 44 Irresistible Qualities Men Want In A Woman.

https://www.amazon.com/dp/B01MQWI11G